GW01373110

A. DETAIL OF CHINESE SIXTEENTH-CENTURY BOWL
LINEAR MAGNIFICATION × 17
See pp. 44, 112

Chinese and Japanese Cloisonné Enamels

by
SIR HARRY GARNER

FABER AND FABER
London & Boston

*First published in 1962
by Faber and Faber Limited
3 Queen Square London WC1
Second edition 1970
Reprinted 1976 and 1977
Printed in Great Britain
at the Alden Press, Oxford
All rights reserved*

ISBN 0 571 04739 4

© *Harry M. Garner, 1962 and 1970*

To
HILDA

Foreword

The genius and inventiveness of the Chinese people have been responsible for many crafts which have enriched western civilisations. The manufacture of silk was one of the first of China's gifts to the west, to be followed by many others, such as porcelain and lacquer. These are all very familiar to us, but we are less aware that there were a few crafts in which the flow of knowledge was from west to east, and not from east to west. The craft of enamelling was one of these. Enamelling was introduced to China in two stages, first in the fourteenth century, in the form of cloisonné enamels, and later on, in the early eighteenth century, in the form of painted enamels. Although the Chinese made important contributions in both these crafts and in some respects surpassed the achievements of the west, enamels were always regarded in China as of foreign origin.

Thus a study of Chinese and Japanese enamels would not be complete without a broad survey of the origins of enamels in the west and of the types which may have influenced the early stages of development in China. This survey, although subsidiary to the main objective of the book, has proved perhaps to be the most difficult task, and it could not have been done without the generous assistance of specialists in the various western civilisations. Among these, I should like to thank especially Mr. R. A. Higgins for information on the Greek enamels, including the earliest enamels of all, the Mycenaean, Mr. D. B. Harden on the Celtic enamels, Professor D. Talbot Rice on the Byzantine enamels, and Professor D. Storm Rice and Mr. R. H. Pinder Wilson on Islamic enamels. I must, however, take the responsibility for any imperfections in the presentation of this material, in which the balancing of views from many sources has not been easy.

In the field of Chinese and Japanese art I am greatly indebted to Dr. Joseph Needham, Mr. Soame Jenyns, Professor S. Howard Hansford, Mr. William Watson, Mr. B. W. Robinson and particularly to Mr. Basil Gray, the Editor of the Series, whose help, indeed, has been invaluable over the whole field covered by the book.

Contents

Foreword	page 1
Preface to the Second Edition	7
The nature of enamels	13
The Early History of Enamels in the West	17
Chinese Enamels in the pre-Ming Period	28
Methods of Assessment	37
Chinese Enamels of the Fifteenth Century	50
The Ching-t'ai Myth	60
The Sixteenth Century	67
The Transitional Period	78
The Ch'ing Dynasty	87
Japanese Cloisonné Enamels	96
Appendix 1	107
Appendix 2	111
Bibliography	114
Index of Authors	117
Subject Index	118

Illustrations

Colour Plates

A. Enlargement of detail from piece of sixteenth-century dish — *frontispiece*

B. Cup-stand. Hsüan-tê mark and period — *facing page* 50

C. Vase. First half, fifteenth century — 54

D. Vase. First half, sixteenth century — 68

E. Box and cover. Early sixteenth century — 72

F. Dish. Wan-li mark and period — 76

G. Vase and cover. Ch'ien-lung mark and period — 92

H. Sword guard. Japanese, nineteenth century — 102

Monochrome Plates
at the end of the book
(the references are approximate)

Western enamels	plates 1–4, 6, 7
Chinese fifteenth-century wares	10–29
Chinese sixteenth-century wares	8, 9, 30–49
Chinese seventeenth-century wares	50–65
Chinese eighteenth-century and later wares	66–84
Japanese wares	5A, 85–94
Marks	95, 96

Where no collection is named for a piece illustrated, the piece is from the author's collection.

Preface to the Second Edition

Since the first edition of this book was printed in 1962 there has been a good deal of interest in East-Asian cloisonné enamels and particularly those made in China. Much new material has come to light since then and it might have been hoped that this would throw some further light on the outstanding problems of identification. These hopes have not been fulfilled, and in particular the major problem of the identification of the earliest wares is still unsolved.

We can have no doubt that Chinese cloisonné enamels were first made in the Yüan dynasty and that they were introduced from the west. The evidence derived from the *Ko-ku yao-lun* was, at the time of publication, a little tentative, because Sir Percival's great work on the *Ko-ku yao-lun* was still incomplete. It has now been completed and his *Chinese Connoisseurship: The Ko Ku Yao Lun, The Essential Criteria of Antiquities*, a translation made and edited by Sir Percival David, is expected to be published this year. The translation of the section on cloisonné enamels given on p. 31 of this book, although it differs in some details from that given in Sir Percival David's book, is by good fortune sufficiently close to need no alteration.[1]

Unfortunately no examples of cloisonné enamel with any solid claims to be earlier than the fifteenth century have yet been found, although Bushell gives factual evidence of the existence of a number of pieces with marks of two reigns of the Yüan dynasty, Chih-yüan (1335–40) or Chih-chêng (1341–67), some of which he saw himself in China.[2] One of these pieces was exhibited at a meeting of the Peking Oriental Society. Not a single piece with one of these marks has since been found, and we do not know whether the pieces belong to the period of the mark or not. Nor have any unmarked pieces been found which might be thought to precede the standard fifteenth-century pieces, such as those illustrated in Colour Plates B, C and Plates 10 to 20. The *kuei* incense burner in Plate 21B, among those ascribed to the fifteenth century, seems to be in a different class from the rest. The enamels are in the same simple colours, and the blue enamel has the violet tinge typical of the group, although much disintegrated. The tendency for the blue enamels to disintegrate is noticeable in other pieces, although not to the same extent. The form and decoration of the *kuei*,

[1] Except that it should be added that five colours of enamel are specifically mentioned. The date of publication of the first edition is 1388 and not 1387.
[2] S. W. Bushell, *Chinese art*, Vol. II, 1910, p. 75.

PREFACE TO THE SECOND EDITION

however, are quite different from those of the rest of the group, with *tao t'ieh* masks and dragons in the style introduced during the Sung dynasty in imitation of the archaic bronzes of the Shang and Chou dynasties. A great deal of the design is in champlevé, only the dragons and a few other details being in cloisonné. It is just possible that this *kuei* may belong to the fourteenth century, if not to the Yüan dynasty, but more evidence would be needed before this view could be accepted. The Ching-t'ai mark has been incorporated in a most ingenious manner, by spinning on to the original base another one with a cast mark (see Plate 95H). The new base includes the bottom flange, and it would seem from a study of the form that the proportions would be improved by the removal of the flange.

One of the most important of the fifteenth-century pieces is the fine dragon jar and cover illustrated in Plates 12, 13. At the time of publication I was unaware that the inscription in champlevé enamel *Yü-yung-chien tsao*, translated as 'made under supervision for imperial use', had a wider significance. The *Yü-yung-chien* in fact was a department of the *Nei fu*, the imperial household, responsible for the manufacture, care and maintenance of objects made for imperial use.[3] This department is known, from the *Ta Ming hui-tien*, 'Statutes of the Ming dynasty', to have been set up by the emperor Hung-wu in 1367, the year before he came to the throne, and to have had a staff of nearly 3000 in the tenth year of Chia-ching (1531). Further study of the *Ta Ming hui-tien* will no doubt bring to light more information on the organisation of the *Yü-yung-chien* and its various sub-departments. A number of other pieces are known, mostly in lacquer, that bear the mark of *Yü-yung-chien* or one of its sub-departments the *T'ien-shih-fang*, Department of sweetmeats. As far as the lacquer is concerned, we cannot be certain that any of the marks are contemporary with the piece. In some instances the marks were certainly added later, no doubt for inventory purposes. But in the cloisonné enamel jar the mark, in champlevé, is set in the enamel and must be contemporary with the piece. The jar must therefore have been ordered by the *Yü-yung-chien*.

Since the first edition of this book was published another jar, an exact pair to that in the British Museum, has come to light. It came from the Summer Palace in 1900 and is now in the collection of Dr. P. Uldry.

One of the most important early pieces that has been found in the last few years is the fine oviform vase fitted with an unusual flanged neck, illustrated in the new Colour Plate C. The decoration of lotus scrolls and petal borders are in conventional fifteenth-century style, but the eight Buddhist emblems, arranged in two bands of four round the neck, separated by a raised gilt-bronze band, is a feature not previously noted in the early cloisonné enamels. The emblems are also to be

[3] I am indebted to Miss Margaret Medley for the information given here on the *yü-yung-chien* and its sub-departments. See her review in the Bulletin of the School of Oriental and African Studies, University of London. Vol. 26.

PREFACE TO THE SECOND EDITION

found in blue and white porcelain and in carved red lacquer of the first half of the fifteenth century.

The suggestion that there is no basis in fact to support the tradition that the Ching-t'ai period was the golden age of Chinese cloisonné enamel, put forward in Chapter 6, has naturally aroused much interest. The view that there are no pieces of Ming cloisonné enamel with a contemporary Ching-t'ai mark was reached after an intensive study and it was not until a few months before the book went to press that I had to discard the last few pieces, which certainly belonged to the fifteenth century, as having had the Ching-t'ai mark added. The ingenuity of the Chinese craftsmen in fitting false bases to genuine pieces of Ming cloisonné enamels is, I think, unprecedented in the Chinese decorative arts. There can be no doubt, as I have said, that an 'organised scheme of forgery on a large scale' was introduced, probably as late as the end of the seventeenth century. There are few records on cloisonné enamel in the Ming and early Ching dynasties, and it would be of great interest to trace the first occasion on which the reign of Ching-t'ai is mentioned. We are unlikely, for obvious reasons, to find positive evidence of when the modifications began to be made. But the facts are inescapable. Since this book was published I have seen many more pieces with the Ching-t'ai mark, but have found none earlier than the end of the seventeenth century with a contemporary mark. No further information has emerged on the five pieces with the Ching-t'ai mark in the Chinese Imperial Collection exhibited at the International Chinese Exhibition of 1935–36,[4] but it is hoped that they will be published before long with full details of the method of construction. It is curious that there is no record of pieces in this collection, now the National Palace Collection in Taiwan, which bear the Hsüan-tê mark, although, as I have pointed out, we now have firm evidence that pieces were made for the Palace by the order of the Yü-yung-chien. One of the dragon jars already mentioned is reliably reported to have come from the Summer Palace in 1900 and the other almost certainly came from the same source.

The absence of contemporary literary evidence and of pieces with reliable marks has been, and will continue to remain, a distinct handicap to the student of cloisonné enamel. There are three reliable landmarks, the fifteenth-century group with contemporary marks of Hsüan-tê, the late sixteenth- or early seventeenth-century group with the mark of Wan-li incorporated in the enamels and the eighteenth-century group with the mark of Ch'ien-lung, in some of which the rose enamel derived from gold is found. In between these groups there are two intervals, each of about 150 years, in which we have to rely on stylistic and technical features for our information on the date of manufacture. It is fortunate that there are so many changes in these and that there were no attempts, as far as we can tell, to copy the earlier wares until we come to the eighteenth century. Although a few

[4] See p. 64.

PREFACE TO THE SECOND EDITION

pieces with the incised Chia-ching mark, such as those in Plates 38 and 39B, cannot with certainty be attributed to the period, they have consistent characteristics which make a Chia-ching dating highly probable.

The pieces with the Wan-li mark in the form *Ta Ming Wan-li nien tsao* are, as I have said, of great importance in establishing one type of cloisonné enamel made in the late sixteenth, or possibly early seventeenth, century. Since the first edition of this book was published a number of other pieces have come to light and it would seem that the manufacture of this group was on a large scale. Several more dishes of the type shown in Colour Plate F are among these, but there are also boxes, bowls and a large square *ting* incense burner, now in the Krolik Collection. An unusual six-sided multiple box in the Metropolitan Museum, New York also belongs to this group. The uniform characteristics, particularly evident in the enamel colours, suggest that all the pieces were made in the same factory and over a limited period. The factory must have had imperial support, in that a number of the pieces are decorated with five-clawed dragons. The use of the term *tsao* instead of *chih* on imperial pieces is rare and may suggest a loss of imperial control as the Ming dynasty was approaching its end.

The question of the provenance and date of the famous enamel mirror in the Shōsō-in, dealt with at length in Chapter 10, still remains controversial. There has been some discussion with Japanese authorities, but no new information has been revealed on the date of its acquisition by the Shōsō-in, and there seems to be nothing in the records to rule out the possibility that it was acquired in the seventeenth or eighteenth century. Miss Blair, whose detailed description of the mirror is referred to in Chapter 10, has since repeated her view that the mirror was made in the eighth century and stated her disagreement with the view put forward in that chapter.[5] There appears to have been a change of view on the provenance of the mirror among Japanese authorities, who now incline to the view that the mirror is of Japanese and not Chinese manufacture.

I do not agree with Miss Blair's views supporting an early date and I can see nothing in what I said in Chapter 10 that needs alteration, in our present state of knowledge. Mr. Basil Gray's views supporting an early seventeenth-century date draw attention to the need for further study of Japanese seventeenth-century enamels. Apart from the sword guards of Plates 88B and 88C, and possibly that of 88A,[6] no examples of seventeenth-century Japanese enamels are included in the book. There are a large number of door and screen fittings in Japan made of champlevé enamel, which seem to have good claims to belong to the Momoyama period, but these are hardly represented in western collections nor, as far as I know, have they been studied by any western

---

[5] See her letter in the *Journal of Glass Studies*, Vol. III, 1963, p. 156.

[6] This may well be earlier than the date suggested on p. 102.

PREFACE TO THE SECOND EDITION

authority.[7] It is not possible at this stage to say more about these enamels, but I realise that the treatment of the Japanese enamels of the seventeenth century is incomplete and needs further amplification. The Japanese enamels of the late eighteenth and nineteenth centuries, particularly those of the types illustrated in Plates 92 and 93B also need more attention. There will probably be sufficient material before long to justify a separate book on the Japanese enamels.

The printing of the second edition of this book has enabled some minor errors in the first to be corrected, but no attempt has been made to alter the text in any other way. The more important new points that have arisen since 1962 have been dealt with briefly in the earlier part of the Preface. Some comment is called for on the figure of a dancing girl in Plate 4B, which was included to illustrate one stage in the development of western enamels. This figure, thought to be part of the crown of Constantine Monomachos, now in the Budapest Museum, has been described by Kurz as 'one of the best and most deceptive counterfeits ever produced'.[8] This view, however, is not accepted by authorities in the Victoria and Albert Museum, who believe the piece to be a genuine Byzantine enamel of the eleventh century. It is rare to find dancing girls in Byzantine art, but it may be noted that they occur in the famous Islamic dish at Innsbruck illustrated in Plates 6, 7, which is almost contemporary with the Byzantine plaque.

Two additional colour plates have been included in this edition. The first (Colour Plate C), has already been mentioned. It is the most important piece of the fifteenth century that has come to light in recent years. The second is an attractive *mei-p'ing* vase, belonging to the first half of the sixteenth century and decorated with grape vines on an unusual deep cobalt-blue ground (Colour Plate D).

H.M.G.

---

[7] A recent publication in Japanese by Yoshimura Motoō, *Shippō* (cloisonné), Kyōto, 1966, describes and illustrates in colour and monochrome a large number of these fittings and other objects, many of which belong to the Hosomi Collection. In addition to the champlevé pieces, in which a dark turquoise enamel is predominant, there are a number of other pieces, mostly in cloisonné enamel, which seem to be later than the seventeenth century. The different types do not appear to be classified or dated.

[8] Otto Kurz, *Fakes. A handbook for collectors and students*, 1958, pp. 217–218.

1. The Nature of Enamels

The term 'enamel' was originally used to describe a hard glossy material fired on to a metal base.[1] In modern times the term has been widened to include many forms of protective coverings applied to different materials. For example, any hard durable paint suitable for application to wood or metal is generally described today as enamel. In this book the term is used in its earlier and more limited sense.

Enamels in China and Japan were based on those of Western Asia and Europe, which were introduced to the East in two stages. In the fourteenth century, enamels of the types in which cells are used to contain the enamel pastes were introduced to China and their manufacture became an important craft right through the Ming and Ch'ing dynasties. These are the enamels that form the subject of this book. By far the most common technique in China and Japan was cloisonné, although champlevé and repoussé were also used to some extent in Chinese work. In the early eighteenth century painted enamels, which had evolved in Europe from the earlier types by a long and arduous development, were introduced into China from Europe. These have little connection with the cloisonné enamels and are best treated separately. They are not discussed in this book, except for a few pieces in which the two processes are combined.

There are many processes in the manufacture of enamels, but in all of them a glassy paste is applied to the metal base and the piece is fired at a sufficiently high temperature to melt the paste and cause it to adhere to the metal. The enamel covering is in fact a form of glass and the story of the development of enamels is one of constant struggle by the craftsman to find a method of associating the two materials, glass and metal, so different in their physical properties, in such a way as to form a durable combination. The brilliant results that can be achieved with enamels, perhaps only surpassed by those of stained glass, a somewhat similar combination of glass and metal, must have been a constant spur to the ancient craftsmen, in spite of the difficulties of the process.

Enamels were undoubtedly made in the first place as a substitute

---

[1] According to M.-M. S. Gauthier, *Emaux limousins champlevés des XIIe, XIIIe et XIVe siècles*, 1950, the French term *esmail* or *esmal* was first used in the thirteenth century, being derived from the twelfth-century plural form *esmauz*, itself derived from the Latin *smaltus*.

for precious stones in jewellery. As soon as man was able to manipulate gold he used it to make articles of personal adornment such as necklaces, clasps and brooches. These gold ornaments were often embellished by the addition of precious stones, set in simple settings. Later on, when the ancient craftsmen were able to make glass, coloured glass replaced the precious stones. For example, cobalt-blue glass was a substitute for lapis lazuli, an opaque bluish-green glass for turquoise and a red-brown glass for garnet or carnelian. At first the glass was cut to shape and mounted in the same way as the natural stones, but afterwards it was secured in position by just melting it sufficiently. Later still, cells were prepared into which glass fragments were placed and fired until they melted to form a true enamel.[2]

Although we may presume that the logical pattern of development just described is roughly descriptive of what actually happened, we may be sure that it was not followed very precisely. The genius of individual craftsmen and fortunate accidents no doubt, at times, enabled short cuts to be made. The material evidence which would enable us to follow the various steps is meagre. Moreover it is extremely difficult to find out, from examination of an excavated piece of jewellery, often in an advanced state of disintegration, whether the material is glass or enamel, or indeed whether the glass is secured by melting or in some other way. This uncertainty increases the difficulty of the art student in tracing the various stages of technological progress.

The earliest glass was probably made in the Mesopotamian valleys well before 2000 B.C. By this time the early craftsmen had long been familiar with the working of metals, including bronze. They were able to solder gold and silver. Thus they had in their hands all the materials and techniques necessary for the manufacture of enamels and it is rather surprising that the earliest known examples of true enamelling, from Mycenaean Greece, are six hundred years or more later than the earliest glass. It must be borne in mind, however, that the fragility of enamel work has been responsible for the destruction of a great amount of the early work, and it is still possible that earlier examples than those from Mycenaean Greece will some day be discovered. At first sight we might expect metal objects covered with a hard vitreous glaze to be very durable, but in fact the attachment of the enamel to the metal is never very secure. In pottery and porcelain the glazes are made of materials that have some affinity with the clay from which the bodies are made and in the firing the glaze partially penetrates the body, forming a secure bond. There are, of course, exceptions to this and when, as in some lead glazes, the materials of glaze and body do not match, the glaze is likely to break away. But in enamelled metalwork there is no really firm attachment and the different rates of expansion and contraction of the enamel and metal under hot and cold

[2] The method of melting a glass rod and allowing the molten glass to fall on to a metal base was adopted occasionally, but it is such an unsatisfactory and uncertain method that it is not likely to have been used except on an experimental basis.

THE NATURE OF ENAMELS

conditions put a continual strain on the piece. When, as in cloisonné enamel, the wires are soldered to the base, we have a number of different metals in contact from which we get, under certain conditions such as occur on burial, electrolytic and chemical action which tends to destroy the piece. Thus there is no doubt that enamelled metalwork is particularly susceptible to the ravages of time.

In studying the history of any of the early crafts we find, as indeed we should expect, large gaps which cannot at present be bridged. In enamels the gaps appear to be particularly wide and we shall see, as we come to look into the development of enamels in detail, that from time to time new techniques were evolved, apparently unconnected with the previous techniques, which seem to have come to an end hundreds of years earlier. It is possible that there are connecting links which can no longer be traced. But it is also possible that enamels were invented anew. Any civilization acquainted with the working of metals and the fabrication of glass, both of which need a knowledge of the control of heating operations, could at any time, by a fortunate chance or by intent, have found a method of combining glass and metal to form enamel. The Assyrians, Egyptians, Greeks and Romans, as well as the later civilizations, all had the necessary knowledge from which the development of enamels, in a number of possible forms, could have been a simple step.

Before we try to follow the chequered history of the development of enamels from ancient times it will be of value to look at the various technological processes that have been used. The difficulty of obtaining a secure attachment of the enamel to the metal forced the early craftsmen to enclose the enamels in small cells. There are three ways of doing this. In the first way, now known by the term *cloisonné*, the cells are made of thin wire[3] attached to the metal base. In the early work the practice was almost invariably to attach the wire by soldering, but in late work, and particularly in Japanese cloisonné of the nineteenth century, the wires are secured by temporary adhesives and are finally held in place by the enamel itself. In the second way, known as *champlevé*, the cells are carved out of the solid metal. In the third, known as *repoussé*, the cells are depressions hammered out of the metal sheet. The French terms cloisonné and champlevé go back to the eighteenth century and are well established in our language today.[4]

The terms cloisonné, champlevé and repoussé, as applied to the Chinese and Japanese work that forms the subject of this book, are sufficiently precise as to leave us in no doubt which technique was adopted in a particular piece. But the early craftsmen often used methods that combined these techniques and it may not be possible to describe an early piece in any one of these terms. For example, the earliest enamels known to us are found in Mycenaean jewellery attri-

[3] The term *cloison* has been used to describe both the wires and the cells. In view of this ambiguity the term is not used in this book.

[4] The term champlevé first appeared in 1753. See M.-M. S. Gauthier, Reference 1.

THE NATURE OF ENAMELS

buted to the thirteenth century B.C., in which the enamels are in shallow depressions surrounded by granulation work, consisting of minute gold spheres attached to the gold base by soldering. The technique, with features both of repoussé and cloisonné, could not be described by any of the standard terms.

As a technique champlevé is simpler than cloisonné and one might have expected that champlevé would have been the first type of enamel to be used. In fact, the reverse happened. Cloisonné was used centuries before champlevé. The probable reason for this is that cloisonné is the most economical way of using the precious gold to the best advantage. Thin sheet can be used for the base and the cells can be built up by the addition of thin ribs. In champlevé, on the other hand, much thicker material is needed and the material is wasted as the cells are cut out. Thus champlevé is more suitable for work on a base metal, such as copper and bronze, and so we find that the earliest use of champlevé on a substantial scale is on such metals. In fact, in its earliest developments, cloisonné was the craft of the goldsmith and champlevé of the coppersmith.

The appearance of the enamels is greatly influenced by the type of metal used. Gold retains its brightness after being heated and translucent enamels on gold are enhanced by the reflection of light from the background. Benvenuto Cellini pointed out that the translucent red enamel is particularly effective on a gold base,[5] while it is not suitable for silver. Translucent enamels are not usually effective on dull copper and bronze backgrounds, and so we find that opaque or semi-opaque enamels are generally used. Chinese enamels come almost entirely in this class, except for a special type of enamel on a silver base made during the late eighteenth and nineteenth centuries.[6]

The last class of enamel to be described here is known as *painted enamel*. It was not until the fifteenth century that the enamel workers of Limoges were able to dispense with the use of small cells and cover a large sheet of copper with a continuous layer of enamel. Many different techniques were explored, in France, Italy and other countries of Europe before the true painted enamels were perfected in the seventeenth century. These were the forerunners of the so-called Chinese *Canton enamels*, in which on-enamel painting is applied to a white ground in the same way as enamel glazes are applied to porcelain.

[5] C. R. Ashbee, *The treatises of Benvenuto Cellini on metal work and sculpture, made into English from the Italian of the Marcian Codex*, 1898.

[6] There were a few exceptional pieces made in the eighteenth century with conventional enamels but on a gold background. See Chapter 9.

2. The Early History of Enamels in the West

We have seen that decoration with enamels is the logical outcome of the polychrome decoration that started with inlaid material such as lapis lazuli and turquoise. This was already well developed in Mesopotamia by the middle of the third millenium B.C. The fine and elaborate inlaid boxes, panels, gaming boards and musical instruments found at Ur, in which lapis lazuli, shell, red jasper and gold leaf inlays are applied to a wooden base, are familiar to most students of early art. But the early examples closest to enamels are to be found in Egypt, magnificent gold ornaments inlaid with small pieces of turquoise, lapis lazuli, carnelian and garnet, the inlays being held in position by ribs soldered to the gold base. Two of the most important are a pectoral of Sesostris II (Pl. 1),[1] which was found in the tomb of Princess Sit-Hathor-iunet at Lahun and a dagger of Princess Ita excavated at Dashur,[2] both of which belong to the XII dynasty and can be dated approximately to 1800 B.C. The metalwork of these is identical with that of cloisonné enamel and the term cloisonné has been applied to them somewhat loosely. As far as can be ascertained, there is no evidence of glass inlay or enamels being used at this time, and indeed it is unlikely that coloured glass was available as early as this, particularly the cobalt-blue glass that made such an impact on Egyptian glass making later on, in the XVIII dynasty. Even in this dynasty no attempts seem to have been made by the Egyptians to take the next step and produce objects such as the pectoral of Sesostris II in enamel. It was left for this step to be taken by the Mycenaeans.

Although the Mycenaeans did not rival the Egyptians in glass technology, they were skilful glass workers and made glass plaques pierced with fine holes so that they could be threaded to form necklaces. These plaques are known in cobalt-blue and turquoise, and although we know that some of the materials for their manufacture must have been imported, such as cobalt, the plaques were certainly moulded in Mycenaean Greece, as is testified by the steatite moulds that have been found there.

The earliest enamels are simple pendants and other forms of jewel-

[1] Guy Brunton, *Lahun I, The treasure*, 1920.
[2] Illustrated in Jacques de Morgan, *Fouilles à Dahchour en 1894–1895*, Vol. II, 1903, Pl. VI.

THE EARLY HISTORY OF ENAMELS IN THE WEST

lery in which cobalt-blue enamel is run into shallow depressions surrounded by granulation work. A number of these have been excavated during the present century from graves in the mainland of Greece, and in Crete and Cyprus.[3,4] They are datable to the thirteenth century B.C. But by far the most advanced piece of enamel is a gold sceptre that carries a spherical knob on which sit two hawks (Pl. 2). The knob is decorated with rows of scales in cobalt-blue, turquoise-green and white in alternation, and the hawks' pinions and feathers are decorated in the same colours. This remarkable sceptre, which appears to be in true cloisonné enamel, reaches a standard of technical achievement which was not to be met again for nearly 2,000 years. The blue and green enamels correspond to the glass plaques in these colours and it is extremely likely that the same materials were used for both glass and enamels.[5]

The sceptre was found early in the present century, but the tomb from which it came was unknown until it was revealed by a patient and skilful investigation made by McFadden in 1952.[6] In the tomb were the cremated remains of a king and queen, and as the practice of cremation was unknown in Mycenaean Greece until it was introduced from Western Asia after the sack of Troy, a date of manufacture in the late twelfth century B.C. has been suggested for the sceptre. This date is supported by the styles of bronze and pottery objects also found in the tomb. The sceptre is thus more than a hundred years later than the earliest of the enamels.

The possibility of enamelling having been introduced into Mycenaean Greece from Asia Minor cannot be ruled out. The cultural contacts between Mycenaean Greece and other contemporary civilizations were very close, and Asiatic and Egyptian influence can be found in many Mycenaean decorative objects. The materials used in Mycenaean Greece, such as ivory, lapis lazuli and even gold were imported from Asiatic countries which had had a traditional use in these materials stretching back a thousand years or more. One of the important materials was cobalt, which plays such an important part in the decoration of Mycenaean glass and enamels. It was probably imported in the form of glass ingots, which were then remelted to make the glass plaques and material for enamels. This glass must have come from

---

[3] M. Rosenberg, *Geschichte der Goldschmeide-kunst auf technischer Grundlage, Zellenschmelz*, 1921–4. Unfortunately the descriptions given by Rosenberg of the enamels, in which other colours than cobalt-blue are mentioned, are quite inaccurate.

[4] H. Maryon, *Metal work and enamelling*, 1954, p. 170.

[5] We know a good deal about Mycenaean glass but little about the enamels. The glass, which contains no lead, has a high melting point, round about 1250°C. However, experiments have shown that glass of this kind could have been used as an enamel at a temperature of 850°C, which would be practicable on a gold base. The constitution of the enamels, a question of great importance in the history of enamel development, cannot be finally settled until materials are available for analysis. Under modern non-destructive methods this would present no serious difficulty.

[6] George H. McFadden, 'A late Cypriot III tomb from Kourion Kaloriziki, No. 40', *American Journal of Archaeology*, Vol. LVIII, 1954.

THE EARLY HISTORY OF ENAMELS IN THE WEST

Asia, and the most likely source of supply for the cobalt was Persia.[7] Indeed, Persia is likely to have been the source of supply for Egypt as well as Mycenaean Greece. There is no native cobalt in Egypt and the vast glass-making industry of the XVIII dynasty must have relied entirely on imported cobalt.

In support of the view that enamelling may have been introduced into Mycenaean Greece from Western Asia is the evidence of a parallel development, that of *niello*, in which metal inlays, made of sulphides of various metals, were fired in a manner resembling champlevé, although at a lower temperature. The superb Mycenaean bronze daggers decorated with niello stand head and shoulders above any contemporary work. Frankfort[8] has put forward arguments, based on a metal belt found at Boghazkuey, that niello was invented in Syria round about 1800 B.C. Although the decoration of the Mycenaean daggers shows some Egyptian influence, Frankfort rules out an Egyptian origin for the technique. Other authorities, however, disagree with him on this particular point. But there is general agreement that the technique came from outside and it is reasonable to suppose that enamels were introduced in the same way as niello, with Syria as the most likely source. However, there is no factual evidence to support this view. No examples of Syrian enamel, nor even of Syrian glass of this period, have yet come to light.

No Mycenaean enamels on a bronze base are known. This is surprising when we think of the skilful niello. But enamels on bronze would be less durable than those on gold, and if they were made are more likely to have disintegrated on burial. The references to *kuanos* in the descriptions of decorated bronze armour in Homer's Iliad, and particularly of the shield made by Hephaestos for Achilles are not generally accepted by Greek authorities as meaning enamel. The processes described are more applicable to the working of iron than of bronze, and all that we can deduce, from the works of the early poets,[9] is that a method of decorating metals with inlaid designs was undoubtedly known in early Greek times.

There is a long interval of time before we come to the next enamels known to us. These are to be found in Greek gold jewellery of the sixth century B.C., which is decorated with minute quantities of blue and white enamels enclosed by thin gold wire, a form of openwork cloisonné. The enamels play a minor part in the decoration and seem to have had little influence on later developments.

---

[7] The view has been put forward that cobalt was obtained from the Caucasus in early times. There seems to be no support for this view, either from Russian or British geological experts. The earliest known workings in the Caucasus were started in 1860.

[8] H. Frankfort, *The art and architecture of the ancient orient*, 1954. Recent studies of early metal inlays by A. A. Moss, *Journal of the Institute for the Preservation of Museum Objects*, 1. 49 (1953), suggest that such inlays before the eleventh century A.D. were pressed into position and not fired. If this view is confirmed a considerable re-orientation of opinion on the early Mycenaean inlays will be called for. The argument associating enamels and niello would be correspondingly weakened.

[9] T. B. L. Webster. *From Mycenae to Homer*, 1958.

THE EARLY HISTORY OF ENAMELS IN THE WEST

By this time the Asiatic 'polychrome style' had spread to South Russia and was to lead to important advances in enamel decoration. A civilization highly skilled in the fabrication of gold, silver and copper had been established in the Kuban as early as 2,000 B.C. The proximity of the Kuban to the Caucasus, so rich in these metals, was no doubt responsible for this culture, for the contemporary civilization in the region of the Dnieper was characterized by painted pottery with no metalwork. The first evidence of the polychrome style, in which inlays of amber are used, appears in the Kuban in the seventh century B.C. and this was followed by the inlay of other materials by the Scythians and Sarmatians, both considered by Rostovtzeff[10] to be of Iranian origin. The methods of polychrome decoration follow those adopted in Mesopotamia, but the geometric designs are replaced by the so-called 'Scythian animal style', with its lively and realistic representations of wild animals, which has close associations with the art of Central Asia and Siberia. The amount of enamelwork, when it occurs, is relatively small and it has often suffered considerably as the result of burial. It is unfortunate that the gold buckle from the famous Maikop belt, now in the Hermitage, Leningrad, in which a griffon attacking a horse is decorated with inlaid stones supplemented by enamels, once regarded as one of the most important Kuban enamels, is now considered by Russian authorities to be a forgery.[11] There is still, however, substantial evidence of inlaid pieces in gold and silver from the second century B.C. onwards, some of which contain enamel.

The method of polychrome decoration developed in South Russia appears to have had a great influence on subsequent enamel decoration in Europe. By the second century B.C. the Sarmatians had advanced to the west of Russia. They reached the Danube, threw back the Romans, and finally with the Goths over-ran most of Western Europe. Rostovtzeff[12] claims that the art was carried by the Sarmatians to the Rhine, Merovingian France, Spain and North Africa, and even reached the county of Kent in England. If this view is correct the development of medieval enamels in Germany and France stems from this source.

Enamel decoration in Celtic work, which first appears at the beginning of the Christian era, seems to be quite independent of the Sarmatians. But it may have been derived in some way, as is suggested tentatively by Burton-Brown,[13] from the polychrome style of decoration that started in the Mesopotamian valleys more than 2,000 years earlier. Enamel objects, in the form of brooches, clasps and buttons, decorated in champlevé on bronze, have been excavated from many sites in France, England and Ireland, notably at Mont Beauvray in France and Polden Hill and Birdlip in England. A contemporary description of the work by the Roman writer Philostratus (A.D. c. 240)

---

[10] M. Rostovtzeff, *Iranians and Greeks in South Russia*, 1922.
[11] Based on work by A. A. Jessen. This information was communicated by Dr. E. Lubo-Lesnichenko, of the Hermitage, Leningrad.   [12] Reference 10.
[13] T. Burton-Brown, *Early Mediterranean migrations*, 1959.

THE EARLY HISTORY OF ENAMELS IN THE WEST

reads, 'It is said that the barbarians of the ocean pour these colours into bronze moulds, that the colours become as hard as stone, preserving the designs'. This is a clear description of champlevé, a technique that was not known, apparently, to the Romans. However, the Celtic enamels must have owed something to Roman glass-making techniques, for we find, by the first century A.D., not only cobalt-blue enamels closely akin to blue Roman glass, but also pieces of glass mosaic known by the term 'millefiori', derived from thin glass rods melted together and cut into sections, a technique that has always been attributed to the Romans. Fragments of rods have been found at Glastonbury and other places, and it seems likely that the material from which the millefiori sections were cut were supplied from some central source. This source has not yet been located, but it is thought that the technique is more likely to have come from Italy than the more remote parts of the Roman Empire. This type of champlevé seems to have continued for a long period and to have been made over a wide region, but it does not seem to have any connection with later developments in Europe. These, in many forms, scattered over the whole of Western Europe may, as has already been conjectured by Rostovtzeff, be based in the main on Gotho-Sarmatian influence.

The next important development in enamels has generally been attributed to the Byzantines, and it certainly culminated in the fine and delicate miniature Byzantine cloisonné on gold of the tenth and eleventh centuries, much of which is preserved in cathedrals and churches, such as St. Mark's, Venice, as precious religious objects. But this final achievement was preceded by a good deal of earlier work, either in Byzantium itself or elsewhere in Western Asia and Europe. Perhaps the most important of the early pieces, from the light that it throws on the history of the subject, is a gold ewer preserved in a small monastery at St. Maurice d'Agaune in Switzerland (Pl. 3). Alföldi has put forward ingenious and convincing arguments[14] that the ewer, of Carolingian manufacture in the ninth century, was made by incorporating cloisonné enamel panels that came from a sceptre of the late seventh or early eighth century made in Syria or some other Islamic centre of Western Asia. Stylistically the decoration accords more closely with that of Umayyad Syria than of either Sassanian Persia or the Byzantine 'oriental style' introduced during the ninth century. The enamels are partly translucent and partly opaque. The translucent enamels are a bright green, bright cobalt-blue and brown-red. The opaque enamels are white, light blue, brick-red and yellow. The two main panels are decorated with the tree of life, one with lions on each side and the other with griffons. Smaller panels have conventional flower sprays. The enamels are similar to those of Byzantium at its finest period and show a great advance over anything that had gone before.

[14] A. Alföldi, 'Die Goldkanne von St. Maurice d'Agaune', *Zeitschrift für Schweizerische Archaeologie und Kunstgeschichte*, 1947.

THE EARLY HISTORY OF ENAMELS IN THE WEST

Even earlier than the panels of the St. Maurice d'Agaune ewer is a small square enamel plaque decorated with a duck, now in the Cividale Museum, which from the circumstances of its find in a Lombardic tomb has been attributed to the late sixth or early seventh century. The plaque is decorated with a combination of cloisonné and champlevé, and the enamels are green, yellow and red on a turquoise ground. Cecchelli considers that the plaque is of Italian or Byzantine manufacture.[15] If the date of the tomb as given by Cecchelli is correct, and there must be some doubt about this, the plaque would, if Byzantine, be far earlier than any other recorded piece. It is possible that the plaque is of Western Asiatic origin of the pre-Islamic period.

Another piece of considerable interest, although it is thought to be a century or so later than the St. Maurice d'Agaune ewer, is a votive offering, also said to be of Carolingian manufacture, which is now in the Victoria and Albert Museum. This piece is in the form of a cross suspended from a silvered iron ring. The cross is of copper and is decorated with floral panels in cloisonné enamels. This is one of the earliest, if not the earliest, pieces of cloisonné enamel on a base metal.

The few pieces of cloisonné enamel made before the full flowering of the Byzantine enamels of the tenth and eleventh centuries pose some difficult problems. It may be argued that the high standard of these early pieces, in which there is a great variety in the enamel colours, suggests that there was a main centre of manufacture. There is evidence to support a Western Asiatic centre which was possibly, although not necessarily, part of the early Byzantine civilization. On these points there are considerable differences of opinion between experts who have specialized in the study of the civilizations of this period. Unfortunately the paucity of material available for study does not yet enable firm conclusions to be drawn.

But whatever was the early history of this type of enamel, the fine Byzantine cloisonné enamels provide the culminating point. The colours are in great variety. There are an opaque cobalt-blue, sometimes in two shades, light and dark, a translucent green, white, red, yellow, purple and black. They are applied to a background of gold, or more rarely silver, and enclosed with gold wires. There is a good deal of repoussé work in some of the pieces, particularly in the modelling of the figures (Pl. 4B). The wires are closely spaced, sometimes being hidden below the enamel where they are not needed to separate the colours. It would seem that this close spacing was needed to give the piece the desired durability. The designs are either of formal scrollwork (Pl. 4A) or they delineate religious figures or simple religious scenes (Pl. 4B). It is rare for individual pieces to be more than an inch or two across and the reliquaries and covers of books are usually built up from a number of small panels. These miniature enamels shine like

---

[15] Carlo Cecchelli, *Monumenti del Friuli dal secolo IV all'* IX, 1943, Vol. I. Also Yvonne Hackenbroch, *Italienisches Email des frühen Mittelalters*, 1938, mentions the representation of an enamel worn by Justinian in the mosaic in St. Vitale, Ravenna.

jewels against their gold background and represent one of the greatest achievements in the history of enamel decoration.

A contemporary account of the methods used by the Byzantine workers has been given by the monk Theophilus, who is thought to have worked in western Germany, in his *Diversarum Artium Schedula*,[16] ascribed to the late eleventh or early twelfth century. This account of many of the industrial crafts of the time includes a full description of the making of cloisonné. Theophilus describes the cutting of the gold strips, the methods of soldering them to the gold sheet, the preparation of the glass pastes of different colours, the filling of the cells and the details of firing and polishing. He tells us, 'The enamels have to be applied several times until the cells are full. The surface is then ground with various materials until it is so smooth that a dry part of the work cannot be distinguished from a part that has been wetted.' There is no reference to any material other than gold.

The view that a number of enamels found in Western Europe, made from the sixth century onwards, are either of Western Asiatic Islamic origin or were derived from them has already been mentioned. The ewer at St. Maurice d'Agaune provides the most important evidence on this point, although the evidence is indirect, based on stylistic considerations. There is no direct evidence of Asiatic enamels from the country of origin until we come to an important large cloisonné dish on copper which bears an Arabic inscription datable to the first half of the twelfth century. This dish will call for full discussion below. For the present we may look at it, together with a few plaques in cloisonné on gold ascribed to the eleventh century, which were found in Egypt, as providing solid evidence of the manufacture of enamels in Syria, Egypt or some other Islamic centre in Western Asia. Whether these enamels originated in Western Asia, or whether they were derived from Byzantine work is, as we have indicated, a matter on which there are differences of opinion. It may well be that the techniques arose in Western Asia, but that there was a strong cultural influence from Byzantium on the subjects and styles of decoration.

Let us now look at the dated Islamic dish in detail.[17] This dish or basin (Pl. 6), preserved in the Tiroler Landesmuseum Ferdinandeum, Innsbruck, is fitted with loop handles and shows in the interior a central medallion, representing the ascension of Alexander, around which there are six other medallions containing eagles, griffons or lions. Between them are alternate palm trees and dancing girls or acrobats. Round the edge is an inscription in Arabic referring to the Ortokid Prince of Amida and Hisn Kaifa, Dā'ūd ibn Sukmān, who reigned from A.D. 1114 to 1144. On the under side of the dish (Pl. 7) the decoration is similar, without the central medallion. The six medallions contain eagles, griffons, wrestlers and musicians, and are separated by

[16] *Diversarum Artium Schedula*, translated with notes by Robert Hendrie, London, 1847.   [17] M. van Berchem and J. Strzygowski, *Amida*, 1910, pp. 120–6, 348–54.

THE EARLY HISTORY OF ENAMELS IN THE WEST

palm trees and dancing girls. There is a second inscription round the edge in Persian which, as far as is known, has not yet been deciphered. The enamel technique is entirely in cloisonné, with bronze wires and strips soldered on to the copper base. The enamels are turquoise-blue, cobalt-blue, red, yellow and white.

This remarkable dish has naturally been the subject of much discussion and various conjectures have been made as to where it was made. The advanced techniques adopted in its fabrication suggest that there was an established centre of manufacture somewhere in Western Asia, where a number of pieces of this kind were made. But in fact no other pieces are known, either in Western Asia or elsewhere.[18] Berchem and Strzygowski[19] have suggested that the dish was made by Armenians working on the borders of Persia. On the other hand Professor D. Storm Rice, who has devoted much time to the study of the dish, finds in it a number of non-Islamic features. The shape of the dish and the type of handles, as well as a number of details in the decoration, such as the branches that stretch sideways from the bodies of the eagles, have no counterpart in typical Islamic work of the period. Above all, the inscription in Arabic shows evidence of being made by a workman with an imperfect knowledge of the language. Professor Rice is of the opinion that the dish was made by foreign workmen in the Ortokid kingdom, possibly by Byzantines. The results of his studies of the many unusual features of the dish and of the Arabic and Persian inscriptions are awaited with interest.

The importance of the dish to the student of Chinese art lies in the fact that the techniques adopted, as well as the enamels, are very close indeed to those of the earliest Chinese cloisonné enamels known to us. Although there is a gap of over two hundred years between the Chinese and Islamic enamels, it seems likely that the Chinese work arose, in some way, out of the Islamic. At any rate, this is by far the closest connection, in actual material, between Chinese enamels and those of the West.[20]

The next important development on a large scale took place in Europe, towards the end of the eleventh century. This was the manufacture of a type of champlevé on copper, generally known by the term 'Limoges enamels', although the manufacture was widespread over Western Europe. Various conflicting views have been put forward to account for the sudden appearance of champlevé enamels in such widely distributed countries as Germany, France, Spain and England

---

[18] The nearest approach to the dish is an icon in the State Hermitage, Leningrad, recently published by A. V. Bank, *The art of Byzantium in the collection of the State Hermitage*, 1960 (in Russian). This represents St. Theodore slaying the dragon. The enamel decoration is in champlevé and cloisonné on copper. Although the icon shows Byzantine influence it was probably made in South Russia and not Constantinople.

[19] Reference 17.

[20] G. Migeon, *Manuel d'Art Musulman*, 1927, has suggested that the Ortokid dish was derived from a Chinese original. We need not take this seriously, but we can regard it as a tribute to the remarkable similarity of the Chinese and Islamic cloisonné enamels.

THE EARLY HISTORY OF ENAMELS IN THE WEST

within a few years. The tradition that they were first introduced into Germany by enamel workers taken there by Theophano, a Byzantine princess who married Otto II in 973, is not supported by any solid evidence, and there are no known examples of champlevé as early as the tenth century. Certainly some of the earliest champlevé was made in Germany, in the valleys of the Meuse and the Rhine, a few years before the earliest manufacture at Limoges itself.[21] Another theory, put forward by Hildburgh,[22] is that a number of the early enamels claimed for Limoges were actually made in Spain and that this type of enamelling was brought to Europe by way of Spain. If this view is correct, the enamels could well have been introduced by the sea routes from Western Asia. Hildburgh's views are not accepted by French authorities, who seem to support the view that the earliest champlevé was made at Limoges.[23, 24] Many writers have stressed the differences in style and the colours of the enamels made in different places, but these differences seem to be less significant than the similarities. The skilful champlevé carving, the method of treatment of backgrounds, the types of enamel and in particular the method of shading the enamels into each other in a single cell, as for example in the delineation of dresses, are all so close to each other that a common origin for all the work seems most likely.

Buchthal[25] has pointed out the similarity in shape and decoration between the Ortokid dish and the European basins in champlevé known as gemellions. This provides further support for an Eastern origin for the European enamels, although they could still have been transmitted by way of Byzantium.

We also have the theory, already mentioned, that the medieval enamels may have been derived from the polychrome style decoration first brought to Europe by the Sarmatians. But it may well be that the inspiration that led to the setting up of a large enamel industry in Europe owed something to all these sources. Nor must we forget that the manufacture of stained glass on a large scale was introduced at about the same time. The basic materials for these two industries were the same and their association may be much closer than has been suggested previously. This is a subject that needs much further study.

The medieval enamels, making use of a base metal in place of gold, enabled pieces of much larger size to be made than had been possible previously. Although cloisonné was used, to some extent, in some of the earlier pieces, champlevé was essentially suitable for this large-scale work and came to be used almost universally, with the occasional

---

[21] O. M. Dalton, *Catalogue of mediaeval ivories, jewellery, gems and miscellaneous objects bequeathed to the Fitzwilliam Museum by F. McClean*, 1912.
[22] W. L. Hildburgh, *Mediaeval Spanish enamels*, 1936.
[23] M.-M. S. Gauthier, *Emaux limousins champlevés des XIIe, XIIIe et XIVe siècles*, 1950.
[24] E. Rupin, *L'oeuvre de Limoges*, 1890.
[25] H. Buchthal, 'A note on enamelled Islamic metal work and its influence on the Latin west', *Ars Islamica*, Vols. XI, XII, 1946.

THE EARLY HISTORY OF ENAMELS IN THE WEST

use of cloisonné, in fine pieces, for the delineation of the faces and hair of the figures. The basic material was copper, which was thickly gilded after the enamelling was finished. Champlevé was produced on an increasing commercial scale up to the beginning of the fourteenth century, but the later work became very perfunctory in execution. In the early fourteenth century a new type of enamel, known as *basse taille*, was introduced, in which translucent enamels were used over gold, silver or gilt backgrounds carved at varying depths, giving the effect of light and shade. The uneven background provided a key for the enamels and enabled the use of cells that had been necessary hitherto to be partly discarded. Basse taille was first made in Siena, from which it spread rapidly to other parts of northern Italy, France and Spain. Another technique suitable for use with translucent enamels was to build up designs in silver or gold foil under the enamel. This type of decoration was also used in combination with the opaque enamels which succeeded the translucent enamels and became the most important types of the fifteenth and sixteenth centuries.

The first step towards the new opaque enamels was the discarding of the carved background and the use of a traced design to which the enamels were applied with the spatula. This led eventually to a type of enamel known as *grisaille* or *camaïeu*, which is always associated with Limoges. In this a ground of black enamel paste is first prepared (sometimes dark blue or some other dark colour is used instead) and white enamel paste is then superposed. This is carved down to the black ground to delineate the outlines of the design in the same way as in cameo carving, and the piece is then fired. The method lends itself to the representation of portraits and figures with great delicacy. Often a second and even a third application of white enamel paste and further carving with the spatula, followed by firing, is needed before the design is complete. The work is all done with the spatula and grisaille is not, strictly speaking, a painted enamel. But there is often a good deal of thin painted enamel applied after the black and white design is finished, which is fixed by a further firing, and another application of gilding fired at a still lower temperature.

Grisaille was the first type of enamel to be made in which the whole surface is covered with a continuous layer of enamel without the use of cells and it paved the way for the true painted enamels, in which designs in colour are painted on to a smooth previously prepared white ground. The technique of applying a continuous layer of enamel on thin copper sheets was greatly assisted by applying enamel to the back of the sheet as well as the front. This practice, which gives stability to the piece, was adopted in the Islamic Ortokid dish and is almost invariably found in Chinese cloisonné, as well as the painted enamels, whenever thin sheets are used as a base.

The first true painted enamels are thought to have been made at Blois by the goldsmith Jean Toutin (1578–1644) round about 1630, although no examples by this maker have yet been identified. Enamels

THE EARLY HISTORY OF ENAMELS IN THE WEST

by his sons Henri and Jean, and by Jean Pettitot, one of Toutin's pupils and perhaps the best enameller of the Blois school, have survived. The enamelling is confined to miniature work in portraiture and in the decoration of watches. More important, perhaps, in their influence on the Chinese painted enamels are the later productions of Limoges, in which more and more painted decoration was applied to grisaille, and of the *Hausmaler* of Southern Germany, who had developed the method of enamel-painting on pottery by 1680. For the first time we find the rose-pink enamel which was destined to play a great part, not only in the *famille rose* decoration of both porcelain and painted enamels in China, but also in the decoration of cloisonné of the Ch'ing dynasty.

This brings us to the end of the story of the development of enamels in the West. Some of the Western enamels had no counterparts in China, but a study of the complete story of the growth of techniques in the making of enamels in the West is necessary if we are to understand clearly how the Chinese enamels were derived.

3. Chinese Enamels in the pre-Ming Period

The earliest Chinese object that has any claim to be considered as an enamel is a bronze ladle in the British Museum which has been described and illustrated by Jenyns.[1] The ladle is said to have come from Anyang and is attributed to the Shang dynasty. Many bronzes of this period have incised designs filled in with a black material of vegetable origin, probably a form of lacquer. The ladle differs from these in having its design of incised cicadas filled in with a silicious material, coloured red by cupric oxide. The composition of the material is close to what would be expected in an enamel. There is no evidence, however, to suggest that the material was fired in position and the date of manufacture of the piece, not later than the tenth century B.C., is much earlier than that of the first Chinese glass known to us. It seems most unlikely, therefore, that the ladle is an example of true enamel.

The early history of glass in China is still obscure. The Chinese writings do not put the earliest date of manufacture earlier than the time of the Emperor Wu (140–86 B.C.) of the Han dynasty. But there is plenty of evidence that glass was made in China long before this. The archaelogical evidence is unfortunately still scanty, but there is some evidence from tombs, notably one at Hui Hsien,[2] which may be as early as the fourth century B.C. But the strongest evidence so far rests on stylistic grounds and in particular on the closely reasoned arguments of Seligman and Beck,[3] who have compared the designs and methods of manufacture of Chinese eye-beads with those made in the Mediterranean area, from which they were undoubtedly copied. The designs of these at times are so close that the Chinese beads could not be distinguished from the Western ones were it not for the presence of barium in the former. This element is never found, except as a trace, in Western beads.

There are good reasons for accepting the view that the Chinese imported glass in the form of ingots from the West. Although there are a few rare examples of the manufacture of glass vessels,[4] glass was almost always used for small objects, such as beads, moulded plaques imitating jade objects and hemispherical bosses used for inlaid decora-

---

[1] Soame Jenyns, 'The problem of Chinese cloisonné enamels', *Oriental Ceramic Society Transactions*, 1949–50.

[2] W. Watson, *Archaeology in China*, 1960, Pl. 83A.

[3] C. G. Seligman and H. C. Beck, 'Far eastern glass: some western origins', *Museum of Far Eastern Antiquities Bulletin*, No. 10, 1938.   [4] Reference 3.

CHINESE ENAMELS IN THE PRE-MING PERIOD

tion of bronzes[5] and pottery vessels.[6] The total amount of material used for such objects cannot have been large and is comparable with the amount of jade, also entirely imported, used at this time. There would not seem, therefore, to have been any difficulty in importing the glass material. However, it would seem, from the fact that the glass of the Han dynasty and earlier generally contained barium, that the glass was reworked with the addition of native materials. Barium has the effect of increasing the refractive index of the glass, a property that gives added brilliance, and it would seem that the Chinese used barium deliberately, so anticipating European glass-workers by more than two thousand years.

The limited use of glass made by the Chinese is explained by the fact that they had developed hard stoneware suitable for vessels long before glass came on the scene. They were thus not interested in glass as a plastic material, but concentrated on the refinement of their felspathic stoneware, which led to the invention of porcelain. Glass was generally used in China as a cheap substitute for jade and other natural stones. Even as late as the eighteenth century glass in China was rarely treated as a plastic material, but was carved in the same way as jade.

The Chinese term for glass was *liu-li*. In its earlier form *p'i-liu-li* it has been derived by Laufer[7] from the Sanskrit word *vaidurya*, which originally meant a stone of natural origin such as rock-crystal or lapis lazuli. The Emperor Wu, already mentioned, is said to have sent special agents over the sea for the purchase of *p'i-liu-li*. The *Wei lio*, written in the third century A.D., attributes to *Ta Ts'in*, the western orient,[8] ten varieties of *liu-li*, carnation, white, black, green, yellow, blue, purple, azure, red and red-brown.[9] We cannot be certain that a man-made product, and not a natural stone, is referred to here and the range of colours may not be as wide as it appears to be from Hirth's translation. But this reference, together with the many later references to *liu-li*, both as a material and in the form of glass vessels, make it reasonably certain that a man-made glassy material, which could have been used for the manufacture of glass, glazes for pottery and porcelain, and even for enamels, was being imported from the time of the Han dynasty onwards.

From the third century A.D. onwards references to the trade in *liu-li*, the material itself, and to glass vessels became more numerous. The references in the *Chu-fan-chi*[10] to Chinese and Arab trade in the

---

[5] A fine bronze of this type, in the Stoclet Collection, is illustrated in Reference 3, Pl. X.

[6] Basil Gray, *Early Chinese pottery and porcelain*, 1953, Pl. 1B.

[7] B. Laufer, *Beginnings of porcelain in China*, 1917.

[8] The exact identification of *Ta Ts'in* is not easy. The question is fully discussed by Hirth and Rockhill (see Reference 10 below), who associate *Ta Ts'in* with the centre of authority of the Christians in Western Asia. In the twelfth century it seems to have meant Baghdad, which at that time was the point where the trade routes of Western Asia united.

[9] F. Hirth, *China and the Roman orient*, 1885.

[10] F. Hirth and W. W. Rockhill, *Chau Ju-kua, his work on the Chinese and Arab trade in the twelfth and thirteenth centuries, entitled Chu-fan-chi*, 1912.

CHINESE ENAMELS IN THE PRE-MING PERIOD

twelfth and thirteenth centuries are of special interest because they give detailed information about the extensive trade that had been built up between many Arab countries and China. It is likely that most of the Arab countries were not actual makers of glass but simply acted as intermediaries.

From the fifth century B.C. onward the Chinese had the materials and the knowledge of techniques that could have been used for the manufacture of enamels. Bronze vessels and objects of personal adornment such as belt-hooks were decorated with incised designs filled in with gold and silver, and more rarely the decoration was enhanced by the use of glass roundels cemented to the bronze base. But the Chinese do not seem to have gone a stage further and fired glass pastes *in situ* to form enamels, nor even to have introduced the process of *niello*, in which metallic sulphides are used instead of the pure metals and fixed in position by firing.

The famous enamel mirror in the Shōsō-in at Nara, in Japan, has been put forward by many writers as being Chinese and belonging to the T'ang dynasty.[11, 12] The mirror, in the form of a twelve-pointed lotus flower (Pl. 5A), is of silver with gold wires enclosing translucent enamels of dark green, light green and brownish yellow. The mirror has been described, in general terms, in a number of Japanese publications, but by far the most detailed description is that given by Dorothy Blair in an American journal.[13]

There is little support today from any experts in Chinese art for the view that the mirror is of early Chinese origin. The author is of the opinion that it is of late Japanese manufacture and certainly not earlier than the seventeenth century. It has no bearing on the early history of Chinese enamels and detailed discussion on it is postponed until Chapter 10, which deals with Japanese cloisonné enamels.

One other piece has been put forward as a possible Chinese enamel dating from the T'ang dynasty. This is a mere fragment, a gilt-bronze lotus base formerly supporting a Buddhist figure, now in the Kyoto Archaeological Museum (Pls. 5B, C). It is three inches in diameter and inlaid with greyish-blue enamel in the champlevé technique. An enamelled ground has also been sunk into the base, upon which appears a gilt scroll design of waves. The piece has been described by Umehara,[14] who considers that it is Chinese and belongs to the T'ang dynasty. The piece has no historical background and nothing similar is known from Chinese sources. Moreover there seems to be little, in the way of stylistic evidence, to support a T'ang rather than a Yüan or Ming date. As a possible piece of early enamel it is worthy of study

---

[11] H. C. Gallois, 'About T'ang and Ta Ts'in', *O.C.S. Transactions*, 1935–6, Vol. 13.
[12] Reference 1.
[13] Dorothy Blair, 'The cloisonné-backed mirror in the Shosoin', *Journal of Glass Studies*, Vol. II (Corning Glass Centre), 1960.
[14] S. Umehara, *Ryūkin Shippō no Butsuzō Taizahen Shiseki to Bijutsu*, pp. 25–8, 1955.

CHINESE ENAMELS IN THE PRE-MING PERIOD

but it has no connection with the early development of Chinese enamels as we know them at present.

The tradition held by the Chinese themselves is that the manufacture of enamels was introduced into China at the time of the Yüan dynasty. Documentary evidence to support this tradition is given in an early Ming work, published less than twenty years after the fall of the Yüan dynasty. The work is the *Ko ku yao lun*, 'Discussion of the principal criteria of antiquities', written by Tsao Ch'ao and first published in 1387. It gives an account of a wide range of antiquities, including paintings, manuscripts, musical instruments, precious stones including jades, porcelain, enamels and lacquer, as well as many other objects. This famous work, perhaps the most important of its kind written in the Ming dynasty, is best known to us by the quotations of Bushell from the second edition prepared by Wang Tso and published in 1459.[15, 16] This edition, which Bushell tells us was in front of him as he wrote his account, has subsequently proved elusive and the problem of distinguishing it from the many later editions has been difficult.[17] However, for the study of the enamels, the first edition is far the more important and there is fortunately a copy of the first edition from the *I men kuang tu* Collection, of which photostat copies are available in a number of libraries in Europe and America, which may be accepted as authentic.

The first edition of the *Ko ku yao lun* has only three chapters as compared with thirteen in the second edition but, although there are some important additions, the great difference in the number of chapters is caused more by re-arrangement than the addition of new material. The second edition conveniently indicates in the margins the new material that has been added. As far as the section on enamels is concerned, the two versions are identical, except for an added sentence in the second edition. The section is headed '*Ta-shih yao*' (Arabian ware) and the full account, which is very short, reads, in the first edition:

'The body of the piece is made of copper, decorated with designs in colours made of various materials fused together. It resembles the inlay work of *Fo-lang*. We have seen urns for burning incense, vases for flowers, round boxes with covers, wine cups and the like, but they are only fit for use in the ladies' inner apartments, being too gaudy for the libraries of scholars of simple tastes. It is also called the ware of the devils' country [*Kuei kuo yao*]. In the present day a number of natives of the province of Yünnan have established factories in the capital [Peking] where the wine cups are made which are commonly known as "inlaid work of the devils' country".' This translation agrees very

---

[15] S. W. Bushell, *Oriental ceramic art*, 1899, pp. 650–2.

[16] S. W. Bushell, *Chinese art*, Vol. II, 1910, pp. 70–1.

[17] I am greatly indebted to Dr. Joseph Needham for information about the early editions of the *Ko ku yao lun*. The book in its many editions has been studied in great detail by Sir Percival David, and the reader is referred to his forthcoming book for further information on the subject.

closely with that of Bushell,[18] but his last sentence, from the second edition, which reads 'The similar enamels made now at Yunnanfu are fine, lustrous and beautifully finished' should read 'The similar enamels made now for the imperial palace are fine, lustrous and beautifully finished'. The implication in Bushell's version that enamels were being made in Yünnan in the fifteenth century, when the second edition of the *Ko ku yao lun* was published, is not therefore substantiated.[19]

Chinese scholars generally agree that *Fo-lang* is the old term for Byzantium. The account of the *Ko ku yao lun* suggests that the enamels were introduced into China from two sources, *Ta-shih* (Arabia) and *Fo-lang*. Bushell[20] interprets the passage as meaning that the Chinese were acquainted first with the enamels of *Fo-lang* and afterwards with those from *Ta-shih*, and even suggests a difference of about a century in the dates of introduction. If this is so, it is likely that the former came to China by the overland route and the latter by sea. But what were the differences between the two types of enamel? We have already seen that the development of enamels in Byzantium was closely linked to that in the bordering Islamic countries, so that the enamels reaching China from these two sources would not be greatly different. Both were in cloisonné. But by the time of the Yüan dynasty important developments in Europe, probably greatly influenced by Byzantine work, had produced a type of champlevé with many features different from those of the Byzantine cloisonné. We have to consider the possibility that enamels of this kind had somehow reached China by the overland route.

We know, from the various accounts that have been handed down, of which the best known is that of Marco Polo, how the Mongols encouraged intercourse and trade between themselves and the other countries of Asia and Europe. Europeans of all kinds, Arabs, Armenians, Georgians, Ruthenians and other races were either taken back by the Mongols as slaves after their many conquests, or were encouraged to enter voluntarily the service of the Mongol court. One of the most important accounts of the Mongols is that left by William of Rubruck, a Franciscan friar who went on a mission to the Mongol court at Karakorum on behalf of King Louis IX of France in 1253, the year before Marco Polo was born, and almost thirty years before the Yüan dynasty was set up.[21,22,23] His sober account of his experiences rings

---

[18] Reference 16.

[19] The reference to the workmen from the province of Yunnan coming to the capital for the manufacture of enamels reminds us that, according to the *Ko ku yao lun* (Bushell, *Chinese art*, 1914, Vol. I), this distant province also had at this time a high reputation for the manufacture of lacquer. But no pieces of lacquer or enamel emanating from Yünnan have yet been identified.   [20] Reference 16.

[21] W. W. Rockhill, *The journey of William of Rubruck to the eastern parts of the world*, 1900.

[22] Sir Percival David, 'The magic fountain in Chinese ceramic art', *Museum of Far Eastern Antiquities Bulletin*, No. 24, 1952.

[23] L. Olschki, *Guillaume Boucher, a French artist at the court of the Khans*, 1946.

CHINESE ENAMELS IN THE PRE-MING PERIOD

true and his observations on the topography of the countries he passed through have been found to be remarkably accurate. We may therefore accept what he has to say about the arts and crafts, which is what concerns us here, as being reliable. His references to the work of the goldsmith Guillaume Buchier are of great interest. Ferguson[24] has suggested that the term *Fa Lan*, an alternative form of *Fo-lang*, is a corruption of Guillaume, the Christian name of the goldsmith. He says, 'At any rate the term *Fa Lan* appears for the first time during the Mongol dynasty and there is a great probability that Guillaume Buchier was the first noted man to produce enamel for the court and that the ware took its name from him'.

There is unfortunately no evidence to support the view that Buchier made any enamels. Friar William describes in some detail a number of pieces in silver made by Buchier, including a fountain in the form of a large silver tree,[25, 26] with four lions at the base, each with a conduit through which gushed forth different liquids, such as mare's milk and wine made from rice and mead.[27] The supply of the liquids is said to have been controlled by a man concealed in the base of the tree, who blew the liquids through the different conduits as required. At the top of the tree was an angel with a trumpet, which sounded forth when the liquids were being provided. This type of fountain was a favourite device of the early potentates. One had been made for the Byzantine Emperor Theophilus (829–842), in the ninth century. Although it would have been a physical impossibility for a man to have blown liquid through the pipes, there is no reason to doubt that Friar William's description of the elaborate silver structure and of its operation, as seen by him, was accurate. This fountain, in the construction of which Buchier had fifty craftsmen working for him over a long period, gives us some idea of the opulence of the court. Friar William clearly did not approve of Western Christians working for a heathen emperor, and describes Buchier as a slave, but his position and conditions of work must have been somewhat similar to those of medieval craftsmen in Europe, such as Benvenuto Cellini.

Buchier came from Paris and it is just possible that he had some knowledge of European enamelwork, as practised by the goldsmith. But such enamels on a miniature scale, similar to Byzantine work, had been almost completely ousted in Europe by the so-called 'Limoges champlevé'. These enamels, on copper, are the craft of the coppersmith rather than the goldsmith and would hardly have come within the purview of Buchier. All the evidence we have, including that of the

[24] J. C. Ferguson, *Survey of Chinese art*, 1939.   [25] Reference 21, p. 208.
[26] Reference 22, p.7.
[27] Basil Gray, 'An unknown fragment of the Jāmi'al-tawārīkh in the Asiatic Society of Bengal', *Ars Orientalis*, 1954, has identified a Persian miniature painting of the pavilion at Karakoram that contained this device. Although the miniature was painted some 150 years after the erection of the fountain, the pavilion has a characteristic Chinese roof, a feature not found in any other Persian miniature of the period, and this suggests that the illustration goes back to an original. Two of the lions are seen in the foreground, but they have been supplemented by elephants, perhaps an invention of the artist.

CHINESE ENAMELS IN THE PRE-MING PERIOD

Ko ku yao lun, supports the view that the first enamels to be made in China were on copper, and not on gold or silver. We can be fairly certain that Buchier had no part in the introduction of enamels to China.

Another possibility, although a remote one, which must be mentioned, is that enamels were brought to China by German workers, who, as is well known, were taken away from their homes to China in some numbers. Friar William was very concerned about the welfare of a group of Teuton slaves, as he called them, of whom he had heard from Friar Andrew of Longumeau, who had been a member of a mission that had visited the Mongol court some years earlier. Friar William enquired about them and found that they had been sent to a town called Bolat, where they were engaged in digging for gold and manufacturing arms, both occupations of great importance to the Mongols. Bolat was only three days' journey from Friar William's route, but he was unable to digress from his set route to see them. The Chinese word for Bolat is P'u-la, and we are told that it was visited by the Chinese traveller Ch'ang-tê in 1259, six years after the time when Friar William was in the neighbourhood.[28] Ch'ang-tê describes the houses as being built with clay and with glass windows. Rockhill thinks that the introduction of glass for windows,[29] most unusual for this part of the world, was made by these same Germans. Thus we see that there were at P'u-la a group of workers with a knowledge of metalwork and glass fabrication, the crafts necessary for the manufacture of enamels. There is, however, no evidence that enamels were made at P'u-la.

In fact there is nothing in the recorded history to suggest any connection between the early Chinese enamels and those made in Europe during the twelfth and thirteenth centuries. Paléologue, in a most confusing statement,[30] has remarked on the influence of Western craftsmen on Chinese enamelwork, and compares Chinese workmanship with that of Byzantium, in which 'gold incrustations in the treatment of figures and hands' are used. The technique referred to is purely European and does not occur in Byzantine cloisonné. But quite apart from this particular technique, there is nothing known in early Chinese enamels remotely resembling the European or Byzantine work, with its emphasis on religious figures and scenes. The use of human figures does not occur on any early Chinese enamels known to us. As for the use of gold incrustations for the faces and hands of the figures, this never occurs in Chinese work, except for a small group of pieces made during the Ch'ien-lung period.

When we come to examine the few facts available for actual pieces of Yüan enamel the evidence is not at all conclusive. Bushell tells us[31] that the *nien hao* of Chih-chêng (1341–67) is found underneath the

[28] E. Bretschneider, *Mediaeval researches from eastern asiatic sources*, 1910.
[29] Reference 21.   [30] M. Paléologue, *L'art chinois*, 1887.
[31] Reference 15, p. 566.

CHINESE ENAMELS IN THE PRE-MING PERIOD

feet of pieces which can be accepted as actual productions of the period. He mentions[32] several pieces bearing the Chih-chêng mark 'flanked by a pair of dragons in the midst of an ornamental ground, the whole executed in cloisonné work filled in with different colours'. He also refers[33] to a broken piece with the four-character mark of Chih-yüan (1335–41) which was once exhibited at a meeting of the Peking Oriental Society. Soulié de Morant[34] states that he saw a piece with the Chih-chêng mark in the possession of a Chinese viceroy. The colours of the enamels were black, reddish brown and dark blue.

Unfortunately no piece with the mark of one of these Yüan emperors, nor of any other, is recorded as belonging to any museum or private collector today. Yet there can be no doubt, from the circumstantial evidence provided by Bushell, who was a very reliable authority in matters of this kind, and de Morant that pieces bearing these marks are, or were, in existence. Whether they are of the periods of their marks or not is a matter which must be left unsettled. Of the pieces of cloisonné for which records exist either in China or the West there seems to be nothing earlier than the early fifteenth century, fifty years or more later than the late Yüan marks referred to.

A comparison of the earliest pieces of Chinese cloisonné known to us with the enamels of the West suggests that the only Western piece that has close associations with Chinese work is the Ortokid dish illustrated in Plates 6 and 7. As far as techniques are concerned, the Chinese cloisonné follows very closely those of the dish. Both use cloisonné with bronze wires soldered to a copper base and the enamels are very similar. Even without the evidence of the *Ko ku yao lun* there are sound reasons for deducing that the Chinese cloisonné is based on Islamic work. With this evidence, coming as it does so closely after the end of the Yüan dynasty, the connection can hardly be disputed. Yet it must be admitted that the subjects of decoration and the treatments of detail show little resemblance. The Chinese seem to have taken over a technique without any of the associated details and to have evolved a purely Chinese style which is far superior aesthetically, and in many respects technically, to that of the originals. It is a curious fact that the Ortokid dish is closer to the relatively decadent Chinese cloisonné of the late sixteenth century than to the early fifteenth-century work.

The question as to whether the influence from the West came to China in two separate waves, as suggested in the *Ko ku yao lun*, or not is quite open. There is no other evidence to support this view and we need further information from both Islamic and early Chinese sources. There is no doubt that the vulnerability of cloisonné enamels is responsible for the paucity of examples of early work, but we may well hope for further connecting evidence as time goes on.

---

[32] Reference 16, p. 75.   [33] Reference 16, p. 75.
[34] Soulié de Morant, *L'histoire de l'art chinois*, 1928.

CHINESE ENAMELS IN THE PRE-MING PERIOD

Such is the evidence, scanty and inconclusive, on enamels in China before the Ming dynasty. When we come to this dynasty we are on more solid ground, with evidence based on actual examples in sufficient quantity and variety to enable us to see a clear pattern of development stretching from the fifteenth to the nineteenth century.

4. Methods of Assessment

Before we begin to study Chinese and Japanese cloisonné in detail, it is desirable that we should give some account of the methods of assessment that have been adopted. The determination of the dates of manufacture of cloisonné, and particularly Ming cloisonné, is a problem that has hardly been attempted in the past. It is natural that the first approach to the problem should be based on the experience gained in Chinese ceramics, partly because the materials are somewhat similar and involve similar conditions of manufacture, in kilns or ovens, and also because it is, above all, in ceramics that most students of oriental art in the West have built up their experience. The author is no exception to this general rule.

In Chinese ceramics a vast amount of knowledge has been built up in the West, particularly during the last fifty years. The sources of this knowledge are widespread. First of all we have the knowledge gained from an examination of the pieces themselves. The materials used, the methods of fabrication, the shapes of the vessels and the style of decoration all make important contributions. The marks, and particularly the reign marks of emperors, in spite of the fact that a large proportion of them are apochryphal, provide valuable information. Additional information comes from the results of excavations in China, now being controlled more scientifically than they were in the past. The writings of Chinese connoisseurs and historians, and of foreign visitors to China, particularly of those contemporary or nearly so with the pieces described, although often obscure and conflicting, add further to our knowledge. Finally evidence of great value comes from the vast amount of material exported to other countries. Although the export wares were rarely those of the highest quality, which were restricted to the imperial household, they have probably been our most fruitful source of information, as far as Chinese ceramics of the last six hundred years are concerned. The documentary evidence associated with these export wares is often of a precise kind rarely to be found in the Chinese writings.

In enamels, on the other hand, we have little knowledge from export sources. Enamels in some quantity were certainly exported, as we know from cloisonné vessels to be found in Buddhist temples in Tibet, India and other Asian countries. But none of this material seems to have reached Europe before the nineteenth century and then not directly from China itself but through these other Asian sources. There

METHODS OF ASSESSMENT

is no cloisonné in early European collections such as the Sloane Collection. The fashion among the royal and wealthy classes for Chinese porcelain in the seventeenth and eighteenth centuries, which was extended to painted enamels on copper, the so-called 'Canton enamels', seems to have ignored the contemporary cloisonné. Thus we cannot expect to find any documentary evidence from European sources such as we find in porcelain and lacquer.

Nor does there seem to be any evidence from Asian sources on the export of cloisonné from China to other Asian countries. Although the export of cloisonné for temple use took place over a wide area, the volume of trade must have been small compared with that in porcelain, or even in silk and lacquer. The trade could have been of little commercial consequence to China and we look in vain for any references to the export of cloisonné in the Chinese literature. So little was known of this trade that we find a wide-spread belief, in the nineteenth century, that some of the cloisonné was made in Tibet. There is nothing to support this view, or to suggest that these temple vessels were made in any country than China itself.

The one reference of documentary importance in the Chinese literature is the *Ko ku yao lun*, first published in 1387, which has already been fully discussed in Chapter 3. This throws no light on the actual types of cloisonné manufactured in China, but it is supremely important in establishing how cloisonné enamels were introduced into China at some time during the Yüan dynasty.

Thus we have little external information of the kind that has proved so valuable in the study of Chinese ceramics and we find ourselves confined to the internal evidence that comes from the study of the style of decoration, the shape, the marks and the technical processes used in manufacture. The stylistic evidence, unfortunately, is not so full as that provided by the ceramic wares, because the subjects of decoration are more limited in the enamels. This is particularly true for the earlier cloisonné, in which lotus scroll designs with lotus petal, classic scroll or cloud borders provide the decoration for nearly every piece. There are, however, stylistic points associated with the methods of manufacture which can be of considerable assistance. The most important of these concerns the background decoration.

The early craftsmen of all countries engaged on the manufacture of cloisonné enamels always had to contend with the need to provide adequate support for the enamel. Large unsupported areas were liable to break away and in an open design the background was filled in with scroll work or other decorative devices. This is clearly seen in the Ortokid dish already discussed in Chapter 2 (Pls. 6, 7) where the figures, animals and birds all have double-lined scroll backgrounds. The border of the dish, with an Arabic inscription, has a background of spirals in single wires, very similar to the arrangement in many pieces of Chinese cloisonné of the sixteenth and seventeenth centuries. It cannot be claimed that these scrolls are particularly appropriate

METHODS OF ASSESSMENT

or that they add much to the decorative qualities of the dish. They seem to be mainly utilitarian.[1]

The Chinese craftsmen of the early fifteenth century laid out their designs, generally of lotus scrolls, to fill the whole of their available space. Every leaf and tendril is so placed that the enamel is supported everywhere, and there is no need for a scroll background. In the later pieces, with their more open designs, scroll backgrounds were introduced. If we look, for example, at two typical pieces of the first half of the fifteenth century (Pls. 18, 20) we can see how the designs are well arranged to fit the spaces available. In the box decorated with fruiting vines (Pl. 26B), a somewhat later piece, although still belonging to the fifteenth century, where the design has become more open, the spaces are filled very satisfactorily with tendrils. But the early sixteenth-century box with the same subject (Pl. 40A) has introduced a scroll background that has no relation to the main design. By the middle of the century the background scrolls had become very perfunctory (Pls. 38A, 39B).

We can also get some information from the shapes of the vessels which will help to fix the date of manufacture. Many of the vessels were made for temple use and it is difficult to find parallel shapes in other materials, such as porcelain and lacquer. Moreover the shapes of cloisonné vessels are essentially those associated with metal construction and differ fundamentally from ceramic ones. Nevertheless we shall find a few pieces in which porcelain counterparts, whose dates of manufacture are known, can be of assistance.

Although there are very few of the earlier marks on cloisonné that can be accepted at their face value, the few reliable ones are of outstanding importance. The marks on cloisonné must be examined with particular care. Unlike porcelain, in which the mark, if in underglaze blue, must be contemporary with the piece, or if in enamels, contemporary with the enamel decoration, many of the marks on cloisonné are incised and could have been added at any time. Sometimes the marks are moulded on to bases that are separately made and soldered or rivetted on, and there can be no certainty that they have not been added later. We are left with a few pieces which without question had the mark at the time of manufacture, either moulded on the actual piece or enclosed in the enamel itself. This is a step forward, but unfortunately the practice of using earlier marks was even more prevalent than it was in porcelain. The mark of Ching-t'ai (1450–6) in particular was extensively used during the seventeenth and eighteenth centuries. However we find, on close examination, a small number of pieces with marks which can be accepted. These are of outstanding importance in a subject which has few oases in a vast desert area.

[1] But D. S. Rice, 'The seasons and the labors of the months in Islamic art', *Ars Orientalis*, Vol. I, 1954, discussing scroll backgrounds on metal, shows how they were developed from the plain backgrounds which were used up to the eleventh century. Spiral scrolls do not seem to appear, however, until the period of the so-called 'Mosul school', some 100 years later than the Ortokid dish.

METHODS OF ASSESSMENT

We come now to the study of the techniques of manufacture and we find, fortunately, that many changes took place during the Ming and Ch'ing dynasties which can be used to provide evidence on the dates at which pieces were made. The author has found that, in contrast with ceramics, where many factors are brought into play in the assessment, in enamels the techniques of manufacture provide by far the greatest amount of evidence, and often the only solid evidence at all. This being so, it is important that the different techniques and the dates associated with them should be explained here as fully as possible. Many of the conclusions derive from straight observations of the material and can be readily checked. Others depend on scientific analyses and technical studies that have so far only scratched the surface. In view of the shortage of information of this kind it is not likely that all the conclusions set out here will stand without modification. The most that can be hoped for is that the framework of identification will prove to be broadly sound, and that others will fill in the gaps in our knowledge as more experience is gained.

As we have indicated, the changes that took place in the methods of manufacture of enamels, in contrast with those of porcelain, which changed relatively little during the Ming and Ch'ing dynasties, were considerable. It is clear that some of the changes, at any rate, were caused by the need for more rapid production. The amount of labour needed in the construction of a piece of cloisonné is enormously greater than that needed to make a piece of porcelain and in the days when each piece of wire had to be hammered out of an ingot and cut to shape the work must indeed have been laborious. The additional work in shaping the wires and soldering each piece in position was considerable. We shall see that the processes of manufacture of the wires and the method of attachment to the body of the piece were simplified as time went on and a study of the construction of the piece often reveals information which helps to fix the date of manufacture.

Considerable changes also took place in the types of enamels used and it is not difficult to divide the cloisonné material into a series of groups in each of which the types of enamel are repeated with great regularity. It is another matter at present to place all these groups accurately in historical sequence, although some broad divisions can be made. It is possible that different enamels, and even different techniques, were adopted in factories in different parts of China and that new ideas, introduced in the capital, Peking, or some other main centre of manufacture, took some time to spread to the more distant factories.

In view of the importance of a knowledge of the techniques of manufacture as a means of dating enamels, it is desirable at this stage to explain them, as practised in China, in detail. We are concerned here almost entirely with cloisonné, in which the wires have to be secured to the body of the piece before the enamels are fired. The process of champlevé, in which the design is cut out of the metal and filled with

METHODS OF ASSESSMENT

enamel, was sometimes used in combination with cloisonné in some early pieces, but there is no evidence that champlevé preceded cloisonné in China or was ever used on an extensive scale before the eighteenth century.

The bodies of the cloisonné pieces that are our concern are made either of copper or an alloy of copper with other metals, to which the term bronze is generally applied. The gilded fittings in the form of handles, covers and feet that are often added to enamel pieces are also made of one of these two metals. The alloys used for cloisonné and for the majority of Ming bronzes are not, strictly speaking, bronze at all. It is necessary to clear up this point before proceeding further.

The earliest bronzes, in whatever part of the world they were made, were alloys of copper and tin, and it was not until a later stage of civilization that the use of zinc as a substitute for tin was discovered. The sequence of events in China was similar to that which occurred elsewhere although, as far as we can judge from present evidence, the date of introduction of zinc into China was much later than it was in the West.[2] The early Chinese ritual bronzes of the Shang and Chou dynasties are true bronzes, with copper and tin as their main constituents, lead often being present as well. These bronzes, if they contain zinc at all, do so in small amounts which must have come in as impurities. It was not until the time of the T'ang dynasty, or even later, that zinc was deliberately introduced by the Chinese craftsmen. By the time of the Ming dynasty the practice of using zinc was almost universal. Generally the proportion of zinc is from 20 per cent to 30 per cent and the amounts of tin and lead are small, each not more than 1 per cent. The composition, in fact, is very close to that of modern commercial brass.

Alloys of copper with zinc have a more yellow appearance than alloys with tin and resemble gold, a fact well known to the Romans, who called copper-zinc alloys *aurichalcum*, while copper-tin alloys and copper were called *aes*. The term 'bronze' was derived from Brundisium (Brindisi) and appears in a fourteenth-century Greek manuscript in St. Mark's, Venice, in the form $\beta\rho o\nu\tau\acute{\eta}\sigma\iota o\nu$. But in English the word 'brass' (A.S. *braes*) is the one that has been in use from medieval times for all kinds of copper alloys. This is the word used by Chaucer and in the Authorized Version of the Bible of 1611. In modern technology and commerce, however, the term 'brass' is generally confined to alloys of copper and zinc. The term 'bronze' is not so precisely used, and although it includes, as its most important group, alloys of copper and tin, it has been extended to include a number of other alloys such as 'aluminium bronze', an alloy of copper and aluminium, and 'manganese bronze', which is essentially a copper-zinc alloy with small amounts of other metals, including manganese, added

---

[2] See a short paper by the author, 'The composition of Chinese bronzes', *Oriental Art*, Vol. VI, No. 4, 1960, for a brief account of the materials used in bronzes of all periods. But there is a good deal of further material awaiting publication.

METHODS OF ASSESSMENT

to give strength. We may sum up by saying that the term 'brass' is used today for an ordinary, every-day material, while the term 'bronze' is reserved for a superior alloy. It would seem not unreasonable to continue the use of the term 'bronze' to describe any copper alloy used for the fabrication of works of art, even although the composition is sometimes very close to that of modern commercial brass. It would indeed create havoc in our nomenclature to do otherwise and in what follows the term 'bronze' will be used for copper alloys with any substantial amounts of other metals and the term 'copper' when the pure, or nearly pure, metal is used.[3]

Most of the earliest cloisonné pieces known to us are made with bases of cast bronze. It was thought at first that the composition of the bases, used in combination with evidence from Ming bronzes, might help to throw light on the dates of manufacture. However, analyses of a few pieces of cloisonné which could be fairly accurately assigned to the first half of the fifteenth century and of some later pieces showed that by the fifteenth century the composition of the bases had become standardized, with 20 per cent or more of zinc as a constituent, with little changes thereafter. No useful evidence therefore can be obtained from the composition. The bases of pieces belonging without question to the fifteenth century show imperfections in the casting, with small blow-holes. It would seem that the standard of bronze casting was not very high at this time. This is in direct conflict with the view generally held in China that the Hsüan-tê period was one in which bronzes of exceptionally fine quality were made. There are many bronzes of fine quality bearing the mark of this period, which have been accepted as early Ming wares. The evidence of the cloisonné pieces suggests that a re-appraisal of these bronze pieces is needed. We may well find that they belong to a much later period than that of the mark.

The early pieces of cloisonné are invariably heavy. One reason for this has been mentioned, the use of cast bronze bases. Another reason is the thickness of the enamels, much greater than we generally find in the later cloisonné. But a warning should be given to those collectors who assume that heaviness by itself is a sign of early manufacture. Many later Chinese wares, enamelled on clumsy cast bases and exceptionally heavy, are among the worst examples of enamelled wares made at any time or in any country.

In the early sixteenth century cast bases began to be replaced by bases built up from metal sheet. Thin sheets, generally of copper, were hammered into shape and soldered together to form the base. Thus we find that dishes, bowls, boxes and even more complicated shapes, such as vases and ewers, were invariably made in this way. A few of the shapes, such as the three-legged incense burner (*ting*) continued to be cast. In order to give strength and stability to pieces made of thin sheet the usual practice was to apply the enamel to both sides of the surface.

[3] Small amounts of other elements often occur as impurities. These are seldom more than one or two per cent of the total.

METHODS OF ASSESSMENT

Bowls and dishes were almost invariably treated in this way. In vases, where it is impracticable to enamel the whole of the interior we frequently find the insides of spreading lips enamelled. Boxes are not enamelled inside, as they are in late Ch'ing times, but they are sometimes lacquered to give extra stability. Bronze sheet is sometimes, although rarely, used in place of copper but no doubt copper was preferred because of its greater malleability. There is no evidence from the pieces themselves to support the view that the adherence of the enamels to a bronze (i.e. modern brass) base is less secure than it is to a copper base.

The wires used in Ming cloisonné are invariably of bronze, and all exposed fittings such as the rims of bowls and dishes, the dividing strips often used as borders to the designs, and such fittings as handles are made of the same material. The Ming craftsman in his selection of material was quite meticulous and went to great pains to ensure that no copper was visible in the finished piece. In bowls with foot-rims the inside of the rim is sometimes enamelled as well as the outside, and in these bowls the foot-rim is sometimes made of copper. But if the foot-rim is to be left unenamelled inside it is always made of bronze. The fact that copper is used at all in a Ming piece is difficult to discover unless the piece has suffered damage.

The use of bronze for all fittings and wires continued throughout the Ming dynasty but in the second half of the seventeenth century bronze began to be replaced by copper. This drastic change was almost certainly associated with the introduction of new methods of manufacture of the wires, which we shall discuss later. By the end of the century the change-over from bronze to copper was virtually complete. As the wires and exposed fittings, whether of bronze or copper, were always gilt at the time of manufacture, the appearance of the newly made piece was hardly affected by the composition of the wires. But when the surface is rubbed and the gilding is removed the material of the wire is revealed. The brightness of Ming cloisonné under worn conditions is in marked contrast with the dullness of the later wares when the copper is exposed and surely justifies the conscientious selection of material by the early craftsmen.

There are a few exceptions to the use of copper wire and fittings in cloisonné of the Ch'ing dynasty. There is a special group of pieces imitating Ming cloisonné in which bronze wires are used. These can easily be distinguished from the Ming originals, as can the Chinese and Japanese copies of the nineteenth century. Apart from these and a small special group made on a gold base and with gold wires[4] the whole of the eighteenth-century cloisonné, including the imperial wares bearing the mark of Ch'ien-lung, make use of copper.

Mention has been made of the laborious method of manufacture of the wires from ingots adopted in the early periods. The method introduced later, of drawing the metal through a die, greatly reduced the

[4] See Chapter 9.

METHODS OF ASSESSMENT

amount of work involved, and it also produced wires of more even thickness. Evidence of the method of manufacture of the early wires is provided by the tendency of the wires to split. The wires in the cloisonné of the fifteenth and sixteenth centuries are always found to include examples of 'split wires'. In some pieces only a few wires are split, but in others a large proportion of the wires are split over the whole or a part of their length. The satisfactory explanation of the splitting has come from a brilliant piece of investigation by members of the staff of the College of Aeronautics, Cranfield.[5] The bowl on which the first experiments were made is illustrated in Plate 31B. It is a typical sixteenth-century piece, decorated with Buddhist lions and embroidered balls on the outside, and inside with galloping horses above waves surrounding a central panel containing a four-pronged *vajra*. The design of the bowl, the enamels used and the other characteristics suggest that it was made not later than the middle of the sixteenth century. In Plate 8 is shown a part of the external surface of the bowl magnified four times. The splitting of the wires is seen clearly, about half of the wires being split in one way or another. In Plate 9 a small part of the surface is shown under a higher magnification, about thirty times. Here we can see the cracks in more detail. One wire, in the centre of the picture, is split from end to end, while the crack in the upper wire comes to an end some distance before the end of the wire. Colour photomicrographs showed something which had not been suspected before, that there was enamel in the cracks, evidence that the cracks were present before the piece was enamelled. This ruled out an earlier idea that the splitting was caused by subsequent corrosion. Colour Plate A, with a magnification of about seventeen times, shows enamel in the cracks of the long wire encircling the mass of turquoise-blue enamel. The reddish tinge of the enamel in the cracks and round the edges of the wires is undoubtedly caused by chemical action of the copper in the wires on the surrounding enamel. In the reducing action of the furnace an effect similar to that of the well known *sang de boeuf* glaze is reproduced.

Studies of photographs taken at a number of positions on the bowl and visual examination of other pieces made it almost certain that the splitting of the wires was accidental, caused by some defect in the method of manufacture. But the splitting of some of the wires was so regular that some experts thought that the wires were deliberately bent over or that double wires were used. It was necessary to dispose of these alternative explanations, and further experiments were made on a second bowl, also belonging to the sixteenth century. The results of these experiments fully supported the views arrived at from earlier tests. A full account of the experiments and the conclusions reached

[5] I am indebted to Professor A. J. Murphy, Professor A. J. Kennedy and Mr. A. R. Sollars for the sequence of experiments which resulted in the solution of the problem. The results have not yet been published. See Appendix 2 for a fuller account of the experiments.

METHODS OF ASSESSMENT

from them is given in Appendix 2. Broadly speaking, we may say that the split wires are caused by the hardening of the material that occurs during hammering. It is well known that constant annealing between the stages of hammering, if properly done, can prevent the cracking, and there can be no doubt that the Chinese craftsmen in the Ming dynasty were aware of the importance of annealing. The fact that some pieces show less split wires than others suggests that there was some variation in the degree of annealing adopted. But the correct annealing treatment needs a great deal of knowledge and attention to detail and while this can be provided under modern accurate process control it is unlikely that the Chinese craftsmen possessed either the knowledge or facilities for perfect control.

The absence of split wires in the later Chinese cloisonné may be explained by the introduction into China during the early seventeenth century of the technique of drawing wires through dies. The technique, derived from the West, is described in a Chinese book, the *T'ien kung k'ai wu*, published in 1637.[6] The method would be particularly suitable for copper wire, much softer than the bronze wire used in the earlier cloisonné, and it may be conjectured that the introduction of the new process and the new material would have taken place at about the same time. Study of actual seventeenth-century pieces, however, suggests that the introduction of wire-drawing came before the change-over of the material from bronze to copper, although more evidence is needed to establish this positively.[7] What is reasonably certain is that both changes took place during the second half of the seventeenth century. The question is further discussed in Chapter 8.

Another technical feature in the manufacture of Chinese cloisonné that changed a great deal as time went on is the method of attachment of the wires to the base. In the earlier work solder was always used. Indeed the earliest pieces suffer from an excess of solder, which often creeps up round the wires and fills in the sharp angles of the designs. It would seem also that the temperature of the enamelling in the earliest pieces was often as high as the melting point of the solder, so that excess solder bubbles through the enamel, causing discolouration and sometimes even leaving globules of solder on the surface. In later Ming pieces there does not seem to be so much excess solder, although the bases of these pieces, when exposed, are often found to be completely covered with a thin layer of solder.

The alternative method of using an adhesive of vegetable origin that burns up in the heat of the enamelling process, leaving the wires to be held in place by the enamel, seems to have been introduced into China sometime during the late seventeenth or early eighteenth century. As

---

[6] But there is some evidence that the technique, applied to iron and steel, was used earlier than this, particularly for the manufacture of steel needles for the mariner's compass. I am indebted to Dr. Joseph Needham for this information.

[7] It is possible that metallurgical examination of seventeenth-century pieces would throw further light on this problem.

METHODS OF ASSESSMENT

far as we can tell by examination of pieces the method of using adhesives does not seem at first to have ousted completely the use of solder, and it is possible that both methods were sometimes used on a single piece. By the eighteenth century solder was rarely used. Moreover it is exceptional to find solder at all in Japanese cloisonné. The method of using adhesives, while it has some advantages in ease of production, leaves the piece very vulnerable to accidental damage. Slight knocks tend to cause the enamel to break away, carrying the wires with it. Cloisonné in which the wires are secured by solder is much more sturdy and if damage to the enamel does occur the wires still remain firmly attached to the base.

The feature of Chinese cloisonné that shows the greatest variation, as we pass through the Ming and Ch'ing dynasties, is the colour scheme of the enamels. It is comparatively easy to divide the cloisonné into groups, in each of which the characteristics of the enamels and other features are similar, but it is more difficult to place the groups in exact chronological order. But by making use of every piece of evidence which can be extracted from such few marks as are reliable, from stylistic features and comparisons with porcelain and lacquer counterparts we can build up a logical pattern of development extending from the first half of the fifteenth to the early nineteenth century.

The enamels of the first half of the fifteenth century are simple, consisting of turquoise-blue, invariably used for the background, dark green that sometimes appears almost black, cobalt-blue, red, yellow and white. These all have their distinct shades, slightly different from those of the later periods, and the only colour calling for special comment is the cobalt-blue, of slightly violet tint, which has a brightness and purity not found again in Ming cloisonné, and only approached in the Ch'ing dynasty. This was almost certainly made from the imported 'Mohammedan blue', as will be explained in the next chapter. This enamel is often sufficient by itself to establish a fifteenth-century date of manufacture.

Later on, and we cannot say yet how early in the second half of the fifteenth century, other colours were used to supplement the simple palette just described. The first new colours consist of a semi-translucent purple, rather pale at first, and the first of the so-called 'mixed colours', consisting of large fragments of paste of different colours fired so that they are joined together, preserving their identity, but not completely fused into each other. This particular colour consists of red and white fragments, and is the so-called 'Ming pink', which served as the only pink until the rose-pink enamel derived from gold was introduced in the early eighteenth century. These colours were followed, at the end of the fifteenth century or perhaps at the beginning of the sixteenth, by a mixed colour consisting of fragments of yellow and green, and a paler green than the dark green of the early period.

In the early sixteenth century further new colours were introduced. These include a turquoise-green and a semi-translucent brown which

METHODS OF ASSESSMENT

seems to have been formed by completely fusing together red and yellow pastes. The cobalt-blue, such a feature of the early fifteenth-century cloisonné, generally becomes dull and greyish, and is used only to a limited extent. By the middle of the sixteenth century more complex mixed colours were in use, sometimes as many as three separate pastes being used for a single colour. By the end of the century we find the introduction of mixed colours in which the fragments are so finely divided that they are hardly visible to the naked eye. The seventeenth century saw perhaps the most complex colour schemes, with a bewildering variety of mixed enamels, sometimes with as many as four colours in combination in a single cell. Towards the end of the century there was a tendency for the colours to become more simple, no doubt the result of the standardization imposed when imperial control of the manufacture was introduced round about 1680. In the early eighteenth century the introduction of the rose-pink enamel derived from gold transformed the colour scheme. Other new colours were brought in which tended to be paler and less effective than the earlier ones.

Mention should be made of the practice of using two enamels of different colours in the same cell. This occurs in the earliest Chinese cloisonné, as can be seen in Colour Plate B. It is derived from Western enamels and is found, for example, in the twelfth-century Ortokid dish,[8] where the treatment of the scrolls is very similar to that adopted in fifteenth-century Chinese work. In some examples the colours show a sharp line of division but in others they blend into each other. This arrangement must not be confused with the true mixed colours.

This necessarily incomplete description of the various enamels will need amplification when we come to discuss particular pieces. It may sometimes happen that some of the enamels appropriate to a particular group are omitted, so that identification becomes more difficult.

Before leaving the subject of enamels we must mention the composition, although it has only a remote bearing on the problem of assessment. There is no doubt that the quality of the turquoise-blue in Chinese cloisonné of all periods is the feature that contributes, more than anything else, to its attractiveness. It has never been excelled in the enamels of any other country. The Japanese, for example, were never able to produce a good turquoise-blue until the late nineteenth century, so that the earlier Japanese vessels always have a sombre appearance. The reason for the excellence of the Chinese turquoise-blue is revealed by recent analyses of a number of differently coloured enamels from two sixteenth-century pieces. All the enamels, with the exception of the turquoise-blue, contain large amounts of lead, the composition being similar to that of crown glass. But the turquoise-blue contains very low amounts of lead, in one instance only 1 per cent, as compared with 20 per cent for other enamels. It is known that the presence of lead in a turquoise glaze has the effect of making it greenish

[8] Pls. 6, 7.

METHODS OF ASSESSMENT

and the best turquoise-blue glazes, such as we find in Persian pottery, are alkaline glazes free from lead. Although the Chinese were well aware of the adverse effects of lead on the colour, they sometimes had great difficulty in getting the pure turquoise-blue they desired on their porcelain. Their knowledge seems, however, to have been applied with success to the manufacture of the enamel pastes. An interesting point is that the adhesion of the turquoise-blue enamels is always excellent, quite as good as that of the other enamels. This is in conflict with the views of some modern Western enamellers,[9] who have maintained that lead is an essential component of enamels if good adhesion is to be obtained.

An attempt has been made, in this chapter, to define the characteristics of Chinese and Japanese cloisonné enamels which can be used to determine the date of manufacture. The methods of assessment laid down are those on which most of the conclusions reached later on in this book are based, and any value which the book may have is derived almost entirely from this approach. Indeed, as has been pointed out, the evidence from other sources is so slight that opinions based on them alone are almost valueless. The subject of Chinese cloisonné, as we have seen, differs enormously from that of the contemporary Chinese porcelain, in which evidence from many sources is available. The multiplicity of sources has its own difficulties and one can observe a tendency among writers on porcelain, when the evidence from the many sources is conflicting, to indulge in conjecture. The author himself has been tempted, at times, to use this intuitive approach. But there is no place for it in a subject so little explored as Chinese and Japanese cloisonné.

Nevertheless, the student of Chinese and Japanese cloisonné enamels has to face the balancing of the evidence derived from each characteristic of a piece. Generally no great difficulty arises in doing this, but there are a few groups in which there is conflict which cannot be resolved entirely on the present evidence. For these groups it has been thought best to give all the relevant evidence with the tentative conclusions derived from them, so that the reader can, if he wishes, check the assessments made by the author. It is hardly to be expected, in a subject which has been so little studied, that there are no errors of assessment, and time alone will show how serious they are. But the broad methods adopted, based almost entirely upon the study of the pieces, are thought to be entirely sound. There has been far too little study of the actual material in the past. For example, it is astonishing that the simple fact that all the Ch'ien-lung cloisonné was made with copper wire and not bronze seems to have escaped the notice of all previous writers on the subject. Here, an ounce of practice seems to be worth a ton of conjectural theory.

* * * * *

[9] H. H. Cunynghame, *Art enamelling on metals*, 1901.

METHODS OF ASSESSMENT

The complex account of the development of cloisonné techniques given in this chapter has been necessary to provide a broad framework for the serious student of the subject. But for those who do not wish to go into the details of technique too deeply a few simple rules for identification are given below. They are necessarily over-simplified and, as in other branches of Chinese art, there are few rules to which an occasional exception cannot be found. But the student new to the subject will find the rules useful until he has gained more experience.

1. Bronze wires and fittings were always used in Ming cloisonné, being replaced by copper from the second half of the seventeenth century onwards.

2. The early wires were made by hammering from ingots and the wires generally show longitudinal splitting. Wire drawing was adopted some time during the seventeenth century and split wires rarely occur after this.

3. The earliest colours are plain and simple. Coarsely mixed colours were introduced during the late fifteenth and early sixteenth centuries, and were replaced by finely mixed colours during the late sixteenth and early seventeenth centuries.

4. The decoration of the earliest pieces is well spaced and no use is made of background scrolls and spirals to fill vacant spaces. The open designs of the sixteenth century often use scroll backgrounds.

5. The rose-pink enamel derived from gold, the so-called *famille rose*, was introduced early in the eighteenth century.

6. The absence of solder is a sure indication of lateness, and is a good means of distinguishing late Chinese and Japanese copies of Ming wares from the originals.

5. Chinese Enamels of the Fifteenth Century

In spite of the evidence of Bushell and other writers on Yüan enamels,[1] no examples of enamels which can be attributed to an earlier period than the fifteenth century are known to us. A group of pieces has now been established, however, which can be attributed with complete confidence to the fifteenth century. The pieces are remarkably consistent in their methods of construction, styles of decoration and in the types of enamels used. Some of them are stylistically close to pieces of porcelain belonging to the fifteenth century and also to lacquer with good claims to belong to the same period. Finally, a few of them bear the mark of the Hsüan-tê period which must, by the fact that they are set in enamel, be contemporary with the piece itself.

The characteristics of cloisonné at different periods have been dealt with at some length in the chapter on methods of assessment. It is necessary to examine once more the characteristics of the fifteenth century pieces in detail, even at the risk of some repetition. The salient technical characteristics of the earliest cloisonné are the use of a cast bronze base, very fine wires shaped and placed with great skill and precision, a good depth of enamel and colours of simple types. These are used to delineate simple designs, almost always confined to lotus scrolls and borders of clouds, leaf and fungus scrolls, and the like. Lotus scrolls form a prominent feature in cloisonné decoration of all periods but a close study of them shows considerable changes in detail design from period to period. In particular the fifteenth-century scrolls are quite different from those of later Ming times. The earlier scrolls are designed so as to cover the available space, so that no subsidiary scroll-work is necessary to fill in the background. The close designs of fifteenth-century cloisonné are paralleled by the designs of fifteenth-century lacquer in which floral scrolls, set against a plain yellow background, almost fill the whole space. In the sixteenth-century lacquer the designs were more open, so that it was necessary to decorate the background with brocade and other patterns. These correspond to the scroll backgrounds of sixteenth-century cloisonné. We shall draw attention to the differences in treatment of fifteenth- and sixteenth-century lotus scrolls when we come to consider individual pieces.

Of the technical features, the construction of the piece itself is the first thing to be studied. In all the early pieces the construction of the

[1] Chapter 3.

B. HSÜAN-TE MARK AND PERIOD. DIAMETER 7·6 in.
See pp. 53–4, 109

metal base, almost always of cast bronze, was completed before any enamel was applied. Thus we find, for example, that the enamels run over the junctions of the handles and feet with the body, giving the piece a completeness and integrity not to be found in later pieces, in which the handles are often added after the enamelwork is finished. If the handles of a piece are found to interrupt or cover the enamel decoration we can be certain either that the piece is later than the fifteenth century or, if it is an early piece, that the handles are a later addition. Many fifteenth-century incense burners have handles of simple shape decorated in champlevé and it may be said generally that the early metalwork is simple in style.

The enamel colours of the earliest cloisonné comprise a turquoise-blue that is sometimes rather pale, a beautiful lapis lazuli blue slightly tinged with purple, a dull red that sometimes approaches a chocolate colour, yellow, white and a dark green that is often almost black. The lapis lazuli blue, derived from cobalt, requires special mention, for it has a brightness not to be found again in Chinese cloisonné until the seventeenth century. We know that the earliest Chinese blue and white porcelain relied entirely on the pure cobalt ore imported from Persia[2] for the blue colour and that it was not until the second half of the fifteenth century that the native impure ores, liable to give a greyish tint, began to be used. The importation of the 'Mohammedan blue' from Persia continued, at infrequent intervals, throughout the Ming dynasty, but it was very precious and there was only enough of it for the most expensive imperial porcelain. Meanwhile some success was being achieved in refining the native ore, and by the seventeenth century good blue colours were being obtained from it. In cloisonné, we have no positive evidence on the composition of the enamels as we have on the blue and white porcelain, but it seems likely that the 'Mohammedan blue' was available for the fifteenth-century wares but was too valuable to be used later for cloisonné.[3] Certainly the ordinary wares of the sixteenth century have a very dull blue and even in the best wares the colour never approaches that of the fifteenth century.[4]

In a few pieces which belong to this group, but may be slightly later than the rest, there is a beautiful semi-translucent purple and an enamel consisting of rather coarse fragments of red and white pastes,

---

[2] See the author's 'The use of imported and native cobalt in Chinese blue and white', *Oriental Art*, Vol. II, No. 2, 1956.

[3] Since this chapter was written, some evidence that 'Mohammedan blue' was used in the manufacture of cloisonné in the fifteenth century has come from analyses of a number of pieces. These analyses, made by the Research Laboratory for Archaeology, Oxford, showed that three pieces, those illustrated in Plates 17A, 26A, and 27A, 27B have small amounts of manganese and were therefore made from imported cobalt, while two sixteenth-century pieces had large amounts of manganese and were made from native cobalt.

[4] It should be mentioned that the cobalt-blue enamel appears to be particularly susceptible to corrosion and if the piece has been badly treated the enamel becomes eroded and discoloured.

CHINESE ENAMELS OF THE FIFTEENTH CENTURY

fused together sufficiently to adhere but not melted into each other, which is the earliest example of the so-called 'mixed colours'.

Another feature of these pieces is worthy of mention. A large amount of solder can be observed at the junctions of the wires and at the sharp bends. In places the solder has tended to ooze through the enamel, causing some discolouration, particularly in the turquoise-blue. Sometimes we can see small globules of solder actually suspended in the surface. No doubt the solder is also responsible for a certain amount of pitting. As has already been mentioned,[5] this effect is no doubt caused by the temperature of the firing of the enamels being above that required to melt the solder.

While we are discussing the technical features of these early enamels we should mention two further points. The presence of pin-holes, which varies according to the conditions of firing, is a feature of Chinese enamels of all periods. The tendency is for the pin-holes to be smaller in size in the later periods. There can be no doubt that these pin-holes were filled in immediately after the firing with suitably coloured hard wax or other material, which has generally, in the earlier pieces, deteriorated and left visible flaws which would not have been tolerated when the piece was new. The question as to how far these defects should be rectified in old pieces of enamel is a matter of opinion. There is something to be said for judicious restoration.

The second point concerns the gilding of the exposed metal surfaces. It is reasonably certain that all Chinese cloisonné of quality had the metal surfaces gilded after the completion of the enamel work. Observation of Ming cloisonné shows that, almost invariably, much of the gilding has worn away and that many of the early pieces have been regilded. This is revealed by the fact that the gilding often covers pieces of wire that have been bent over by damage and cavities that have not been filled in properly before regilding. The effect is sometimes unsightly and should warn us against attempting to regild pieces of Ming cloisonné, particularly when they have suffered damage.

This enumeration of the features, mainly of a technical nature, which enable us to identify this early group must not cause us to overlook their high aesthetic appeal. The designs, mainly of lotus scrolls, cloud scrolls and other formal ornament, in their simple, almost primary, colours are clear cut and striking. A brief glance at the corresponding eighteenth-century designs, evenly and mechanically disposed, with a more complicated colour scheme, shows how inferior these latter are. The fifteenth-century enamels, like the fifteenth-century blue and white porcelain, has certain serious technical defects which were largely overcome at a later period, when mass production methods replaced individual craftsmanship. But the loss of artistry which almost always follows the introduction of mechanical methods associated with a marked increase in production is no less noticeable in

[5] Chapter 4.

CHINESE ENAMELS OF THE FIFTEENTH CENTURY

enamels than it is in porcelain. A close acquaintance with the enamels emphasizes more and more the outstanding qualities of the fifteenth-century cloisonné as compared with the later wares.

Let us now study in detail the actual pieces which can be attributed with some confidence to the fifteenth century. One of the pieces, which has helped perhaps more than any other to establish the identity of this early group is the well-known disc (Pl. 10A), which is thought to have had some ritual significance. It is of cast bronze, decorated in cloisonné with a central lotus seed-pod surrounded by a petal border and clouds. The enamels are in the simple colours of the types already enumerated, in which the dark green is hardly to be distinguished from black. The disc bears round its edge the six-character mark of Hsüa-tê in bronze surrounded by the enamel. The mark is not in cloisonné but in champlevé, i.e. it was either left exposed on the disc in the original casting or was carved out of the solid before the wires were attached. The necessity to fit the wires round the mark has clearly caused a slight distortion of the design in the neighbourhood of the mark.

The design of the disc is close to that of a medallion that decorates the inside of a blue and white bowl in the Chinese Imperial Collection at Taiwan (Pl. 10B). The bowl, unmarked, certainly belongs to the fifteenth century. Mr. Soame Jenyns, who has examined the bowl,[6] thinks that the style of the dragons decorating the outside of the bowl points to a somewhat later attribution than the Hsüan-tê period.

Another cloisonné piece closely resembling the disc is the fine cylindrical box with slightly domed lid (Pls. 11A, B), which has a somewhat similar stylized seed-pod surrounded by petal borders and finally an unusual arrangement of two rings with segments of different colours. The sides are decorated with fungus scrolls. The Hsüan-tê mark, as in the disc, is in champlevé and the cloisonné design has again been slightly modified to take it. Like the disc, the box is made of cast bronze.

Two dishes with raised centres also belong to this early group (Col. Pl. B and Pl. 22). Such dishes or cup-stands, suitable for taking a cup on the raised central platform, are fairly common in blue and white, red and white, white and celadon porcelain of the fourteenth and early fifteenth centuries. No contemporary cups, either in porcelain or cloisonné, are known and this is surprising because the rather earlier Korean celadon cup-stands are often seen with their contemporary cups. It has been suggested that the cups used with the Chinese porcelain and cloisonné cup-stands were made of gold or silver and have not survived. But it must be pointed out that there are two references in the *Ko ku yao lun* of 1387 to wine cups made in cloisonné.

The two cloisonné dishes are of similar construction, the main body being of cast bronze, undecorated underneath, and the central

[6] Soame Jenyns, 'A visit to the Pei-kou, Taiwan, to see early Ming porcelains from the Palace Collections', *O.C.S. Transactions*, Vol. 31, 1957–9.

53

raised platform being made separately and rivetted on before the enamels were applied. In both dishes the central part is decorated with a single stylized flower, surrounded by a narrow petal border on the shaped flange. The dish in Colour Plate B has as its main feature lotus scrolls surrounded by a second petal border and a wave border on the flanged rim. Wave borders of this kind are a common feature of many blue and white fifteenth-century dishes. The cloisonné dish has a six-character Hsüan-tê mark incised on the base, the incision being filled in with dark blue enamel (Pl. 95A). The presence of the enamel makes it certain that the mark is contemporary with the piece.

The second dish has for its main feature a continuous flower scroll with flowers of different kinds, strongly reminiscent of flower scrolls on fifteenth-century dishes in blue and white. Such borders are also to be found in carved lacquer boxes of the early fifteenth century. Scroll borders in the well of the dish and on the flange, both of which can be matched in fifteenth-century blue and white, complete the decoration. The enamels are similar to those in the pieces already mentioned, with the slight addition in places of mixed red and white enamels, introduced to give some shading to the flowers. The dish has a well written six-character Hsüan-tê mark incised in double-lined characters running vertically down the dish (Pl. 95E). Double-lined characters were certainly in vogue before Ming times[7] and the possibility of the mark being contemporary with the piece cannot be ruled out. But the mark, being incised, could have been added later, and we have examples of somewhat similar marks in double-lined characters bearing the *nien hao* of the Emperor Wan-li (Pl. 95F). The presence of the mixed enamel suggests that the dish may be a little later than the three pieces with the mark set in enamel, which may be tentatively accepted as belonging to the period of the marks. Even so, the dish is likely to have been made some time before the end of the century.

The fine large jar and cover bearing the Hsüan-tê mark (Pls. 12, 13A, B, C), decorated with five-clawed dragons on a background of clouds and waves, is probably the most important piece of cloisonné of the fifteenth century to have survived. While there can be little doubt as to its fifteenth-century date, there is some difficulty in accepting it as of the period of the mark. The techniques adopted in its manufacture are very close to those of the pieces already described. The wire-work is finely controlled and the enamels are exceptionally deep, with a thickness of nearly a quarter of an inch. The depth of the enamel suggests that the piece must have been filled in with enamel pastes an unusually large number of times for successive firings, appropriate enough for such a large and important piece. The colours are of the usual simple types, the cobalt-blue being particularly good, with the

---

[7] A number of silver vessels of the Yüan dynasty with marks in double-lined characters are described by Laurence Sickman, 'Chinese silver of the Yüan dynasty, *Archives of the Chinese Art Society of America*, Vol. XI, 1957. Similar characters occur on the lid of the large dragon jar, described below.

C. FIRST HALF, FIFTEENTH CENTURY.   HEIGHT 10·2 in.
Dr P. Uldry

CHINESE ENAMELS OF THE FIFTEENTH CENTURY

addition of a fine rather pale semi-translucent purple and traces of the mixed red and white enamel round the head of each dragon. The dragons are, in the main, bright yellow and against the background of clouds and waves in turquoise-blue, deep cobalt-blue, red, white, and dark green produce a striking effect. The jar bears two inscriptions on opposite sides of the neck, one the six-character mark of Hsüan-tê (Pl. 13B) and the other the mark *Yü yung chien tsao*, 'made under supervision for imperial use' (Pl. 13C). As in the disc of Plate 10 and the box of Plate 11A the marks are in champlevé. There are similar marks on the flange of the cover, incised in double-lined characters. The base material of the jar is sheet bronze, consisting of pieces hammered out and soldered together.

In most respects the qualities of the piece conform to those of the pieces already mentioned as belonging to the Hsüan-tê period. The two factors which suggest a later date are the additional enamels, the purple and the mixed red and white, and the design of the dragon itself. There are important differences in the treatment of the dragon's head from that of blue and white porcelain and lacquer of the Hsüan-tê period, and while these may be in part attributable to differences in techniques in different materials, one would have expected in an imperial piece — and there can be no doubt that the cloisonné jar and cover are imperial — closer agreement than there is. The most unusual feature is the treatment of the dragon's mane, which is divided and spreads on either side of the head. In one of the dragons on the jar one part of the mane flows downwards and the other upwards (Pl. 12) while on the dragon on the opposite side of the jar the two parts of the mane flow upwards. The dragon on the cover (Pl. 13A) shows this latter arrangement. This treatment of the mane is not, as far as the author is aware, to be found on any imperial piece in porcelain or lacquer. The nearest approach to the downswept mane is in the cloisonné bowl of Plate 31A, once thought to be a late fifteenth-century piece, but now attributed to the early sixteenth century.

To sum up the evidence on this piece, it is difficult to be more precise than to say that it belongs to the fifteenth century, with some characteristics that favour a date in the second half of the century. It may very well belong to the Ch'êng-hua period (1465–87).

There are a number of other pieces, either unmarked or bearing marks which cannot be said to be contemporary with the piece, which have qualities so close to those of the marked pieces already discussed that we can certainly ascribe them to the fifteenth century. Several of them bear the Ching-t'ai mark but, for reasons which will be discussed in the next chapter, the marks should be viewed with considerable suspicion. The pieces will therefore be considered, in this chapter, entirely on their merits.

One of the finest unmarked pieces is the large cylindrical vessel (Pl. 15) standing on three bracket feet and decorated with a bold design of lotus scrolls with double-lined stems. The use of such stems is not

CHINESE ENAMELS OF THE FIFTEENTH CENTURY

common in this period, but there are two other examples (Pls. 18, 19A). How different is the treatment from that of the typical eighteenth-century double-lined scrolls, so even and mechanical in their outlines. The finely cast handles in the form of phoenix heads are almost certainly not contemporary. Another fine and unusual piece is the beaker or *ku* (Pl. 18), decorated with double-stemmed lotus scrolls in similar style. The beaker has had a copper-gilt liner, finely incised with stiff leaves, added to the mouth and the base, which bears the incised six-character mark of Ching-t'ai above a four-pronged *vajra*, is also of copper-gilt. Both were probably added during the Ch'ien-lung period. This type of beaker is a popular form in cloisonné and many later Ming examples were made, particularly in the late sixteenth and early seventeenth centuries (Pl. 52), but they are much less sturdy in shape than this fifteenth-century example.

A group of incense burners on three feet (*ting*) and fitted with two curved upstanding side-handles (Pls. 17A, 19A) are typical examples of fifteenth-century work. Four incense burners of this kind are known, of which no less than three were at one time in the Kitson Collection. They are decorated with lotus scrolls and bands of clouds and other formal ornament, and some of them have a horizontal row of gilt-bronze circular bosses in the form of stylized flowers. Impressed bosses of this kind are a familiar feature in fourteenth and fifteenth-century celadons. Although there are some differences in detail in the decoration, all four incense burners are similarly made, of cast bronze, and the handles are similarly decorated in champlevé. The enamels in all four are similar and are confined to the simple colours represented in Colour Plate B. Two of the incense burners have their original covers, each with an aperture in the centre. One of the covers is surmounted by three gilt-bronze rams, (Pl. 17A), a symbol of spring. The second piece has a simpler form of cover and the body is decorated with lotus scrolls with double-lined stems below a row of gilt-bronze bosses separated by clouds (Pl. 19A). This shape of incense burner seems to have been soon superseded by one in which the feet are much shorter and the handles, in loop form, are integral with the mouth-rim. A typical example of this later type, which was the most popular form of incense burner in the sixteenth century, is illustrated in Plate 40c.

Another type of incense burner (*kuei*) found in the fifteenth century is typified by the fine example decorated with lotus scrolls shown in Plate 14. The handles are in champlevé, with cloisonné details. A similar *kuei*, with Ching-t'ai mark (Pl. 21A), which will be discussed more fully in the next chapter, has had a new base added to it. A third piece of this shape, of somewhat later period (Pl. 30A) is of importance in indicating the line of development of this type. It will be discussed in the chapter on sixteenth century cloisonné. Another form of *kuei*, following more closely the old bronze forms of the Shang dynasty from which the shape was undoubtedly derived, is decorated with *t'ao t'ieh* masks and other archaistic motives (Pl. 21B). This, like

CHINESE ENAMELS OF THE FIFTEENTH CENTURY

the *kuei* of Plate 21A, bears the Ching-t'ai mark on a base which was added later.

The beautiful box and cover (Pl. 19B), of bronze cast in the form of a lotus flower and decorated on the top with a lotus seed-pod surrounded by rings of petal ornament and with lotus sprays in the surrounding moulded panels is also an early piece. The decoration on the top closely resembles that on the ritual disc (Pl. 10A) and the colour scheme is similar, except that the green is much paler. On the base is the six-character incised mark of Ching-t'ai in a calligraphy which suggests a later date than the fifteenth century.

The well-known vase with oviform body and slender neck (Pl. 20) is typical in every way of fifteenth-century work. The body is decorated with lotus scrolls and the neck with two bands of stiff leaves separated by a gilt-bronze raised ring. The colours are quite typical although the the turquoise-blue ground is rather paler than usual and the red-brown has taken on a chocolate tinge. The piece bears the Ching-t'ai mark incised on the base in good calligraphy (Pl. 95D). It will be more fully discussed in the next chapter.

The attractive sprinkler or *kundika*, used for the sprinkling of holy water in Buddhist ceremonies (Pl. 16) is similar in shape to bronze vessels of the T'ang dynasty, frequently depicted as carried by deities in pottery and bronze figures of the period. The *kundika* was in regular use in Lamaist ritual in the Ming and Ch'ing dynasties and is often, in Tibetan banners, shown with other objects standing on a table before a deity or deified Lama. The cloisonné *kundika* is decorated with lotus scrolls round the body with petal borders above and below. The spreading foot has a border of inverted petals in gilt-bronze between another inverted petal border and a leaf scroll in cloisonné. The finely engraved foot, which bears also a four-pronged *vajra* on the base is of gilt-copper and is an eighteenth-century addition. The filling aperture at the side, with hinged cover, has a representation of three flaming pearls, with strong Buddhist associations. A libation vessel with spout and ring-handle, decorated with lotus scrolls above a petal border and below a leaf scroll similar to that on the foot of the *kundika* (Pl. 17B) is another fine example of a fifteenth-century ritual vessel. This also has a finely engraved *vajra* on the base.

Most of the pieces of fifteenth-century cloisonné are in shapes suitable for ceremonial use and there is an almost complete absence of domestic wares, such as we find, for example, in porcelain and lacquer. The shapes of the vessels and the almost exclusive use of lotus scrolls for the main decoration support the view that these fifteenth-century pieces were made for Buddhist temples. There are, however, no examples of the use of the more specific Buddhist representations in the decoration such as, for example, the eight precious emblems or the *vajra* in fifteenth-century cloisonné and they are in fact rare in porcelain and lacquer of the period. It was not until the sixteenth century that this kind of ornament was developed.

CHINESE ENAMELS OF THE FIFTEENTH CENTURY

We now come to a group of boxes which show a breakaway from the formal ornamentation found in the mid-fifteenth century wares and the beginning of a naturalistic treatment of flowering and fruiting branches (Pls. 23, 24, 26A, B). Although the main themes of decoration are different the boxes in other respects are so similar that we are justified in concluding that they all came from the same factory, although they may have been made over a considerable period of time. The boxes are of cast bronze, with a shallow and wide foot-rim and a deep flange on the lower part. The decoration of lotus scrolls round the sides is identical on the four boxes. The main subjects of decoration, grape vines (Pl. 26B), persimmons (Pl. 24), pomegranates (Pl. 23) and a formal lotus flower (Pl. 26A) are quite different. The first three boxes have the six-character Hsüan-tê mark thinly incised in a single vertical line both on the base and on the inside of the lid (Pl. 95c). The fourth has an owner's mark thinly incised on the base. The calligraphy of the *nien hao* does not resemble that which we associate with the period, but almost certainly belongs to the sixteenth century or later. The boxes themselves are certainly of fifteenth-century manufacture, but three of them (Pls. 23, 24, 26B) show considerable development in the enamels over the simple palette of the dish in Colour Plate B, and make a late fifteenth-century date likely. An additional pale green enamel, much paler than the usual dark green, which is still retained, has been introduced and the mixed red and white enamel is also used sparingly. In the box decorated with grape vines the semi-translucent purple is appropriately used. There is also a tendency to develop further the method of shading two colours into each other in a single cell, which was used to some extent in the earlier pieces. The persimmon fruits of the box in Plate 24 are of red and yellow, artistically shaded into each other. These, of course, are not mixed colours in the usual sense. The similarity of the design of the persimmon sprays to those on the late fifteenth-century moon vase (Pl. 25) lends additional support to the view that the cloisonné box belongs to the second rather than the first half of the fifteenth century.

One further piece which may be regarded as a borderline fifteenth-century piece must be mentioned. This is a four-sided vase (*tsun*) with simple side handles (Pls. 27A, B), not particularly distinguished in shape but with extremely fine decoration in cloisonné, on one pair of sides with formal lotus scrolls and on the other with freely drawn peonies. The colours are in the usual fifteenth-century palette with a very good cobalt-blue, but with the addition of a pale green to supplement the darker green. The vase probably belongs to the last few years of the century.[8]

Finally, to bring the catalogue of fifteenth-century pieces to a close, there is another group of pieces with qualities quite different from those of the pieces already discussed. These are analogous in shape and decoration to the well-known group of Ming pottery and porcelain

[8] This is one of the pieces in which 'Mohammedan blue' is used. See footnote 3.

CHINESE ENAMELS OF THE FIFTEENTH CENTURY

enamelled on the biscuit and generally described by the term *fa hua*, in which the design is made by threads of clay separating the different coloured enamels. This group, which has for a long time been prized by connoisseurs for its decorative qualities, has always presented some difficulty in dating. The pieces are never marked with a *nien hao*, except for some late pieces with the mark of Chêng-tê. Hobson and other writers of his time considered that the pieces were made round about 1500. In recent years there has been a tendency for much earlier dates to be given, stretching back even to the fourteenth century. But a study of the designs, and particularly the border patterns, show that they conform more closely to those of the blue and white porcelain of the last quarter of the fifteenth century than to any other group. There seems therefore no reason for changing materially the attribution given by Hobson some forty years ago.

The similarity of the cloisonné and porcelain jars shown in Plates 28 and 29 can leave us in no doubt as to the close connection between the two types. The use of threads of clay to restrain the enamels on the porcelain is so close to the use of wires in cloisonné that it is reasonable to assume that the *fa hua* was developed from the cloisonné. The cloisonné pieces in this group, in spite of their simple colours, restricted to turquoise-blue, cobalt-blue, green, yellow and white, do not fit in very well with the rest of the fifteenth-century wares. The workmanship is not so good and the enamels are more roughly applied. The *fa hua* pieces, although the quality of some of them is very fine, are heavier in construction and broader in treatment than the typical Ching-tê Chên wares. Moreover the bodies of these pieces vary from an almost pure white porcelain to a brown, rather soft pottery. It seems likely, therefore, that the *fa hua* wares were not made in the Ching-tê Chên kilns and it is possible that some of them were made at potteries close to the enamel factories where the cloisonné was made. These may have been much closer to the capital, Peking.

The pattern of development in the fifteenth century, as it emerges from our discussions, shows first a group of pieces with a strictly limited palette in the enamels and with designs confined to lotus scrolls and formal borders. A small number of these bear the contemporary mark of Hsüan-tê and may be accepted as belonging to the period. These simple designs were followed by more complicated and less formal ones, associated with an extension of the range of enamel colours, including the first of the 'mixed colours'. There was a tendency for the new designs to become more open, so that scroll backgrounds were needed to support the enamel. All these changes began to take place before the end of the century. Further developments followed, both in the subjects of decoration and the enamels. The story of these developments belongs to the sixteenth century and is dealt with later in this book.

6. The Ching-t'ai Myth

In the last chapter we saw that a group of pieces of cloisonné enamel, with clearly defined characteristics, can be confidently ascribed to the fifteenth century. Some of them, with simpler enamels, belong to the first half of the century. They were followed by pieces with more complex enamels and more open designs, so that by the end of the century new developments of great importance were well on the way. The full story of these belongs to the sixteenth century and is described in the next chapter.

Among the fifteenth-century pieces there are, as we have mentioned, a number bearing the mark of Ching-t'ai. The attribution of these to the fifteenth century has been made on their individual qualities and without taking into account any evidence from the marks themselves. The reason for this is that the evidence of the marks, as the study of the subject has proceeded, has appeared to be more and more untrustworthy. Until recently the author thought that there were a few pieces at least which might be accepted as bearing contemporary marks of the Ching-t'ai period. This view has not withstood a critical examination of the evidence and has had to be discarded.

The absence of any evidence for fifteenth-century cloisonné bearing contemporary Ching-t'ai marks raised the question as to when they were first used on cloisonné, and this focused attention on the later pieces. The conclusion reached may here be stated briefly. There is no evidence that the Ching-t'ai mark was used before the mid-seventeenth century. It follows that the traditional basis of attribution of Ming cloisonné in China, as exemplified by treasured pieces in the Chinese Imperial Collection, is no longer tenable. In fact, the view that the Ching-t'ai period was the golden age of Ming cloisonné is a complete myth.

These categorical statements will require the support of a good deal of factual evidence before they are likely to be accepted. The objective of this chapter is to provide this evidence. But before we do this it is worth while to look at the legend and to make a brief historical survey of the disturbed and undistinguished part of the fifteenth century that lies between the reigns of Hsüan-tê and Ch'êng-hua, the so-called interregnum.

The first thirty-five years of the fifteenth century were years of great prosperity for China. Under the wise guidance of two emperors, Yung-lo (1403–24) and Hsüan-tê (1426–35), the prestige of the country

THE CHING-T'AI MYTH

was high, the Mongols in the north were well held in check and many successful expeditions were made by sea, mostly under the command of Chêng Ho. During this period the arts prospered. Hsüan-tê in particular was a great patron of the arts and his reign has a high reputation for many crafts, including the manufacture of porcelain. On his death he was succeeded by Chêng-t'ung (1436–49), who became involved in a badly planned campaign against the Mongols which ended in the destruction of the Chinese army and the capture of the emperor. He was succeeded by his brother who reigned as Ching-t'ai (1450–6), but when Chêng-t'ung was released by the Mongols he again assumed the throne, Ching-t'ai being deposed, and reigned under the new style of T'ien-shun (1457–64). He was succeeded on his death by Ch'êng-hua (1465–87), whose reign has a reputation in the manufacture of porcelain second only to that of Hsüan-tê.

The period of thirty years from the death of Hsüan-tê to the accession of Ch'êng-hua has been described as the interregnum, a period of little distinction between two reigns of great importance in the history of Chinese art. It must be admitted that the term has arisen mainly in connection with the manufacture of porcelain, but it seems that very little distinction in any field can be given to the three reigns of Chêng-t'ung, Ching-t'ai and T'ien-shun. As for Ching-t'ai, he seems to have taken the throne under compulsion during his brother's captivity and to have been deposed in his favour as soon as the opportunity occurred. On his death, burial as an emperor was refused and his body was interred in an isolated tomb to the west of Peking, in a spot remote from the tombs of the other Ming emperors.[1]

There is little in the history of the Ching-t'ai period to suggest that it was responsible for the development of the manufacture of cloisonné to a standard not approached at any other period. When one thinks of the complexity of manufacture of a piece of cloisonné, requiring the co-operation of a number of different types of craftsmen, it seems likely that the development of techniques up to the standard reached in the fifteenth century would be a long and arduous one. It is most unlikely that any six years would have been responsible for particularly rapid developments and the reign of Ching-t'ai, one of the least distinguished of all the Ming emperors, would seem to be a most unfavourable time for any outstanding advances in cloisonné or any other material. Yet the legend that cloisonné reached a standard during the Ching-t'ai reign that was not approached at any other period became firmly established in China during the Ch'ing dynasty and, as we shall see, the *nien hao* of this undistinguished emperor was used widely on cloisonné of all periods as a mark of distinction. We do not know when exactly the legend was first established, but Bushell has told us[2] that by the end of the nineteenth century the name of Ching-t'ai had become synonymous with cloisonné, which was actually known as *Ching-t'ai lan*.

[1] C. P. Fitzgerald, *China, a short cultural history*, 1935, p. 465.
[2] S. W. Bushell, *Oriental ceramic art*, 1899.

THE CHING-T'AI MYTH

Let us now look at some pieces bearing the Ching-t'ai mark. There are only five pieces recorded with this mark that can be ascribed to the fifteenth century. Two of them have moulded marks and three incised marks. An incised mark could have been added at any time to the base of a piece and the evidence of such marks cannot carry much weight by itself. Moulded marks, which cannot be added in the same way, at first sight seem to be more reliable, but closer examination shows that new bases with moulded marks can be so cleverly added that the additions are very difficult to detect.

The two pieces with moulded marks are both incense burners of the form known as *kuei*. The first of these, decorated with lotus scrolls (Pl. 21A), is very similar in design to the unmarked *kuei* of Plate 14 and there can be no doubt that both belong to the first half of the fifteenth century. The base of the former, which bears the six-character Ching-t'ai mark (Pl. 95G), at first sight appears to be integral with the piece, which was once accepted as one of the very few pieces with a contemporary mark. But a close scrutiny revealed that a new base, carrying a cast mark, has been cleverly superposed on the old base. A comparison of the marked *kuei* with the unmarked one of Plate 14 shows that the shape of the former is less satisfying aesthetically and that the projecting base has made the petal border round the base less effective. But it must be recorded that these apparently self-evident points were only revealed after a close study of the method of fabrication had proved that a new base had been added.

The second *kuei*, of different shape (Pl. 21B), follows more closely the shape of the Shang bronze original from which it was derived. The archaistic designs of *t'ao t'ieh* masks and dragons, far removed from the originals, are similar to those that appear in bronze and jade pieces attributed to late Sung and subsequent dynasties. The cloisonné *kuei*, undoubtedly of fifteenth-century manufacture, bears the cast four-character mark of Ching-t'ai on the base (Pl. 95H). A study of the piece shows that a new base, enclosing the old, has been added in a similar way to that on the *kuei* already discussed. There is actually a space of about one sixteenth of an inch between the new base and the old.

The vase of Plate 20 bears the six-character mark in line along the edge of the base (Pl. 95D). This well-known piece, of fine quality, has been fully discussed in the past by various writers,[3,4,5] and has always been attributed to the Ching-t'ai period. All the features of the vase point to a fifteenth-century date, and it may very well belong to the first half of the century. The evidence from the mark itself is of no value. Quite apart from the fact that, being incised, it could have been added at any time, the base of the piece, made separately and soldered on, is certainly a later addition.

The fourth piece bearing the Ching-t'ai mark is the fine beaker (*ku*),

[3] *Chinese art*, 1935 (chapter on bronzes and the minor arts, by W. W. Winkworth).
[4] Soame Jenyns, 'The problem of Chinese cloisonné enamels', *O.C.S. Transactions*, 1949–50.   [5] *The arts of the Ming dynasty*, 1958.

belonging to the first half of the fifteenth century and decorated with double-lined lotus scrolls (Pl. 18). This has an incised six-character Ching-t'ai mark in line along the edge of the base, above a four-pronged *vajra*. The base, copper-gilt, is clearly a later addition and the piece has also had a liner, made of thin sheet copper and gilt, attached to the mouth-rim. The liner is finely engraved with stiff leaves.

The last piece with the Ching-t'ai mark is the beautiful box in the form of a lotus flower (Pl. 19B). This is undoubtedly a fifteenth-century piece, possibly belonging to the second rather than the first half of the century. The calligraphy of the mark, which is incised in a line along the edge of the base, is not at all typical of the fifteenth century and is probably a very late addition.

A close study of these five pieces convinced the author that at some period after the fifteenth century a deliberate scheme of falsification, based on the supposed superiority of cloisonné of the Ching-t'ai period, was embarked upon. We know that in porcelain pieces of the earlier important reigns, such as Hsüan-tê and Ch'êng-hua, were copied in later Ming and Ch'ing times, with varying degrees of skill. Some of the copies were very good indeed and can hardly be distinguished from the originals, while others are less skilful and are easily recognized. A third category is of pieces made in the style of the period but given earlier marks, clearly marks of commendation. Most of the pieces bearing earlier marks can be accepted as having been made with no intention to deceive, and even with the most accurate copies we may be generous enough to accept the view that these pieces were made to replace breakages from a service and that an attempt was made to reproduce every feature, including such details as the construction of the foot-rim. In the cloisonné with Ching-t'ai marks no such concessions are possible. The addition of incised marks by themselves might be regarded as an expression of opinion by an owner, based on a tradition of the excellence of the Ching-t'ai period. But the highly skilful fabrication of bases with cast marks and their ingenious attachment in such a way that the additions are very difficult to detect indicates a well-planned organization of deliberate forgery.

To find out when this grand deception was first introduced we need to consider marked pieces which are of later periods than the fifteenth century. Before we look at these it should be noted that the additions to the *ku* (Pl. 18) are in gilt-copper, a material not used in Ming work. These additions were certainly made in the eighteenth century. The excellence of the work and the skill of the engraving shows what high standards were maintained in this century. The fact that the additions to the two incense burners are in bronze suggests that they were made before the end of the seventeenth century, but we cannot rule out the possibility of the deliberate use of bronze by eighteenth-century adapters.

There are scores of pieces belonging to the sixteenth and seventeenth centuries which bear the Ching-t'ai mark and we shall now consider some of these. Among them are five pieces in the Chinese Imperial Collection some of which, if not all, are at present in Taiwan. They were included in the International Exhibition held in London in 1935 and are illustrated in the catalogue of the Chinese exhibits.[6] The author has only a vague recollection of seeing these pieces in the exhibition and has not had the privilege of examining them since. His opinions on the dates of manufacture are therefore based on a study of the black and white photographs, liable to be misleading in a subject in which the colours of the enamels and the methods of fabrication play such an important part. However, most of the pieces have their counterparts in Western collections and it is possible to reach firm general conclusions from the photographs alone, although study of the actual pieces would be necessary to enable the details to be filled in.

The first piece to be considered is a deep dish to which have been added three supports in the form of kneeling figures (No. 2034, Pl. 5 of the Chinese Imperial Catalogue).[7] It is similar in the style of decoration to another dish (No. 2005, Pl. 6) bearing the Wan-li mark and undoubtedly of the period. The former dish bears the six-character mark of Ching-t'ai, but the piece belongs to the late sixteenth century.

The other four pieces are vases of various kinds. The first, with a bulbous body decorated with birds on a prunus and bamboo background with formal borders above and below, is in typical early seventeenth-century style (No. 2004, Pl. 1).[8] The base has the moulded six-character mark in the form *Ta Ming Ching-t'ai nien tsao*, the only piece of the five with the *tsao* character, on what seems to be an added base. The second piece is a beaker (*ku*) with grapes on the central section and flower scrolls above and below (No. 2036, Pl. 2). This also has a six-character mark on the base in the more usual form. The piece itself probably belongs to the mid-sixteenth century. The third piece is a leys jar (*cha tou*), with elephant-head side-handles (No. 2006, Pl.4). This, a mid-sixteenth-century piece, has the four-character moulded mark.

The last piece is a lobed flower vase with dragon side-handles, decorated with *t'ao t'ieh* masks and other formal ornament (No. 2035), illustrated here in Plate 46. This has a moulded mark, of six characters, which appears to be let into the base. The enamel decoration is of the type normally associated with the early seventeenth century. It would be necessary to examine the enamels before one can give a more precise date, but it can be said with certainty that the piece cannot be earlier than the second half of the sixteenth century. The elaborate handles may well be a later addition.

[6] *Illustrated Catalogue of Chinese Government Exhibits for the International Exhibition of Chinese Art in London*, Vol. IV, 1937.
[7] For these pieces the number in the main catalogue, and the plate number in the Chinese Catalogue, are given.
[8] It is unfortunate that the descriptions of this piece, both in the main catalogue of the Exhibition and in the Catalogue of the Chinese exhibits, do not agree with the photographs. There are similar discrepancies in other cloisonné pieces.

THE CHING-T'AI MYTH

These five pieces, belonging to the Chinese Imperial Collection, not only have no resemblance to those established as belonging to the fifteenth century but, more important, can be associated with pieces in Western collections which can be dated to the sixteenth and seventeenth centuries. The question as to whether any of the marks are contemporary with the pieces themselves cannot be conclusively settled from a study of the photographs but it seems extremely likely, from such details as can be discerned, that most if not all of the marks are later additions.

Many other Ming pieces bearing Ching-t'ai marks have been studied. Some of them are illustrated in this book and will be discussed later on. While the pieces can be dated, on various grounds, from the first half of the sixteenth century onwards, most of the marks can be seen to have been added later. In a number of pieces the addition of the mark is easily recognized, but in others, such as the two incense burners in Plates 21A and 21B, the addition is more difficult to detect. But the conclusion has been reached that no piece, of the many examined, which has an unquestionably contemporaneous Ching-t'ai mark, can be dated earlier than the mid-seventeenth century. The excellence of the calligraphy of some of the added marks, and the fact that they have been accepted as genuinely belonging to the fifteenth century by Chinese experts, raises grave doubts on the use of calligraphy as a method of dating cloisonné. Undoubtedly the calligraphy of brush work has more subtle qualities than characters moulded or incised on metal and the same doubts do not necessarily apply to marks on porcelain. The question is further discussed in Appendix 1.

Reference should be made here to a group of pieces decorated in Ming style with a ground colour of rather pale greenish-turquoise. A consistent feature of this group is that there is a first application of turquoise enamel over the whole piece, the other enamels being applied on the top of this for a second and subsequent firings. The wires and exposed fittings are of bronze and a careful attempt has been made to simulate Ming cloisonné. But there are a number of features, including the absence of solder, which proclaim that these pieces are not earlier than the late seventeenth century. Some of these pieces have Ching-t'ai marks in cloisonné enamel (Pls. 61D, E). They may very well be the earliest pieces with this type of mark.

It has been established, without any reasonable doubt, that the Ching-t'ai mark was not used on cloisonné until a date long after the fifteenth century. The earliest possible date, on the evidence put forward, is the mid-seventeenth century. The mark came into use as a means of adding lustre to pieces already in existence, rather than being applied to newly made pieces. The question of how the undistinguished reign of Ching-t'ai came to be chosen as a mark of commendation is at present a complete mystery. No references in the Chinese literature are known. But it is certain that, once the idea that the name of Ching-t'ai was one to conjure with had been established, an organized scheme of

THE CHING-T'AI MYTH

forgery on a large scale was introduced, by which bases with well-cast marks were so cleverly attached to the bases of existing unmarked pieces that the additions are very hard to detect. At the same time the practice of adding new fittings in the form of handles and feet began to be introduced, often with disastrous results to the simpler earlier shapes. These additions can be detected by the fact that the cloisonné design has been cut to accommodate them, a practice never to be found in the cloisonné of the fifteenth century.

The addition of Ching-t'ai marks seems to have been made without discrimination, so that we can find them on Ming cloisonné of every period. There are even, as we have seen, among these marked pieces, a few belonging to the fifteenth century. It is a curious fact that the reign of Hsüan-tê, during which a few pieces with contemporary marks were almost certainly made (Pls. 10, 11A, Col. Pl. B), was ignored when the grand deception started and equally curious that, of the pieces holding pride of place in the Chinese Imperial Collection, not a single piece with the contemporary mark of Hsüan-tê is recorded.

The exposure of the Ching-t'ai myth need not cause any serious concern to the student of Chinese cloisonné. He should ignore the marks and concentrate on the qualities of the pieces themselves. The addition of false bases and fittings, reprehensible as it is, was not, fortunately, accompanied by any of the more subtle forms of forgery. In fact no copies of the earlier cloisonné seem to have been made until the eighteenth century, and these late copies can easily be distinguished from the originals. In this respect the collector is in a far happier position than the collector of Ming porcelain, in which excellent copies of the wares of earlier reigns began to be made within one hundred years, and sometimes within fifty, of the death of the emperor.

7. The Sixteenth Century

Although, from a military point of view, the security of the Ming dynasty became steadily worse during the sixteenth century, the country was very prosperous internally. The prosperity was assisted by the continuity of two long reigns, that of Chia-ching (1522–66) and Wan-li (1573–1619). Under these emperors the arts and crafts flourished, particularly in porcelain, lacquer and textiles. In porcelain the production of pieces for the court was on an enormous scale, as we know from the official lists of pieces that have been recorded and the many pieces that have been handed down. In lacquer there is little documentary record, but there are many pieces bearing the reign marks of Chia-ching, Lung-ch'ing and Wan-li which can be accepted as authentic. Textiles, both woven and embroidered, belonging to the same general period but not accurately datable, have survived in some numbers. The decoration of all these pieces, in porcelain, lacquer and textiles, is based on the same motives of dragons, phoenixes and emblems, and reflects the imperial taste of the time.

In cloisonné, there is hardly any material that bears any of the reign marks of the sixteenth century, nor are there more than a very few pieces decorated with imperial subjects. It would seem that there was very little imperial interest in the manufacture of cloisonné until towards the end of the century, when a few pieces decorated with dragons and phoenixes, and bearing the Wan-li mark, were made. The vast amount of sixteenth-century cloisonné, some of which is of fine quality, seems to have been made at private factories.

We have seen that the early cloisonné enamels of the fifteenth century form a remarkably consistent group, with designs and enamels conforming to a strict pattern. Changes in both these features were beginning to take place before the end of the century. Most of the developments were exploited in the early years of the sixteenth century, which saw more rapid changes in cloisonné than there were at any other time in the Ming or Ch'ing dynasties. Thus although the cloisonné of the sixteenth century rarely reaches the standard of the fifteenth, it shows much greater variety. It seems likely that cloisonné was made in a number of separate factories, each with its own styles and techniques, and working to some extent independently of the rest. We have as yet, however, no evidence to show where these factories were situated.

THE SIXTEENTH CENTURY

In the manufacture of porcelain, in which very high firing temperatures are needed, it was economically reasonable that the factories should have been set up in one area. Ching-tê Chên became the centre of manufacture, and although a vast amount of pottery, stoneware and porcelain of one kind or another was made all over China, almost all the high grade porcelain made for the use of the court or the wealthy classes was made at Ching-tê Chên. Its distance from the centre of government in Peking must have caused great inconvenience and an attempt was made in the seventeenth century, in the reign of K'ang-hsi, to set up a centre of manufacture of porcelain in Peking. This was unsuccessful,[1] and the economic factors that had created Ching-tê Chên as the centre of manufacture of porcelain in China have been sufficiently powerful to maintain it in being right up to the present day.

In enamels, on the other hand, the firing temperatures are relatively low and can be achieved by simple means. Among the illustrations prepared by T'ang Ying by command of the Emperor Ch'ien-lung in 1743 to describe the various processes of manufacture of porcelain, one of the illustrations, No. 18, entitled 'open and closed muffle stoves', makes particular reference to cloisonné.[2] It states, 'The open stove is used for the smaller pieces. The stove is similar to that used for cloisonné enamels on copper, and it has a door opening outwards. When the charcoal fire has been lighted inside, the porcelain is placed upon an iron wheel, which is supported upon an iron fork, by which the porcelain is passed into the stove, and the fireman holds in his other hand an iron hook, so that he may be able to turn the wheel around in the fire and equalize the action of the heat. When the colours appear clear and bright the firing is reckoned to have been sufficient.' Such simple stoves as these, needing relatively small amounts of fuel, could have been set up anywhere. A group of skilled metalworkers, supplied with the basic metals and glassy pastes from outside, could have made any of the Ming pieces of cloisonné known to us in a small factory.

While the broad distinctions between fifteenth- and sixteenth-century cloisonné enamel are as we have defined them in Chapter 4, there was of course no sharp transition at the turn of the century. But the arbitrary choice of the year 1500 as the dividing line has much to recommend it. There are strong reasons for thinking that the great changes that distinguish the two types began to take place during the last twenty years of the fifteenth century and had become fully effective within the first twenty years of the sixteenth. We may recall that the two most striking changes were the development of an entirely new range of enamels and the opening up of the designs, which necessitated the introduction of background scroll decoration. It is not easy to substantiate by simple factual argument that these changes took

---

[1] See Chapter 9. It was, however, found possible to set up factories in Peking for the decoration of porcelain with enamels.

[2] S. W. Bushell, *Oriental ceramic art*, 1899. See also Sir Percival David, *Artibus Asiae*, Vol. XII, 1949.

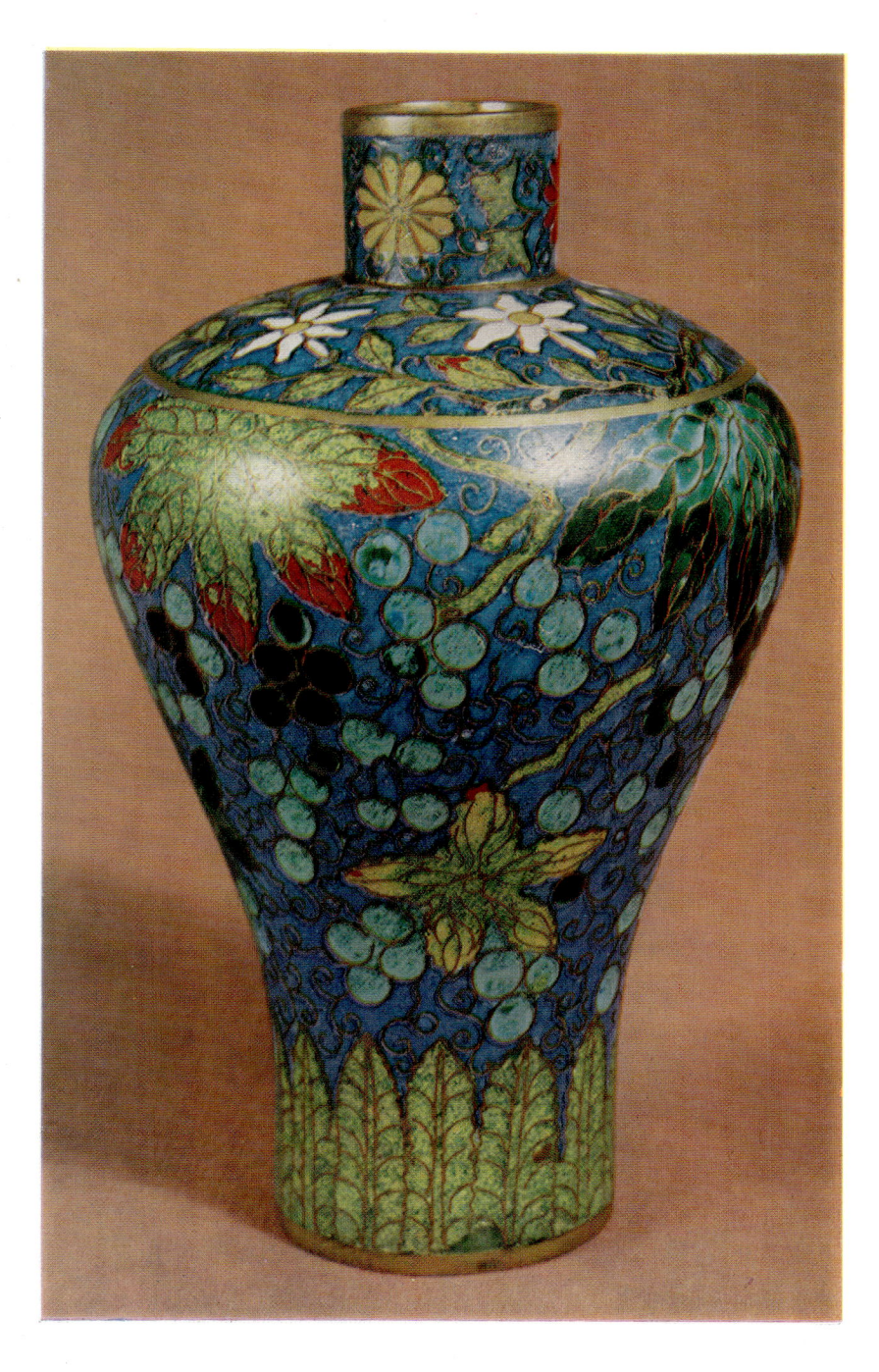

D. FIRST HALF, SIXTEENTH CENTURY. HEIGHT 7·9 in.

THE SIXTEENTH CENTURY

place in such a short time and one must always bear in mind that if, as seems likely, cloisonné was made in a number of places some distance apart, there may have been some delay in new ideas developed at one factory becoming adopted at another. The examples which will be described and illustrated will, however, it is hoped, provide strong support to the general theory put forward here.

An important borderline piece is the incense burner in the form known as *kuei*, decorated with lotus scrolls (Pl. 30A), which is very close to the fifteenth-century pieces already described (Pls. 14, 21A). But the elaboration in the design of the lotus flowers, the crowded arrangement of leaves along the stems, the use of an enamel of different colour in the space between the two stems supporting each flower and other details, combined with the use of purple enamel and an additional shade of green, all suggest a later date. The foot of this piece does not seem to be original. The similarly decorated bowl of unusually deep shape (Pl. 30B) shows some further development in the palette, with the addition of a turquoise green, quite distinct from the turquoise-blue background, and a semi-translucent brown enamel which seems to have been formed by a complete fusion of red and yellow components. This bowl brings us well into the first quarter of the sixteenth century and leads to a well-known group, consisting mainly of bowls, belonging to the first half of the century. Among other features, these pieces often have Buddhist and other emblems incorporated in the design. The deep bowl has a four-pronged *vajra* on the base inside.

A typical bowl in this group is the one that was used for the investigation of the split-wire characteristics of early Ming cloisonné. These were fully discussed in Chapter 4 and it is not necessary to say anything about them here, except to remind the reader that split wires are a characteristic of all fifteenth- and sixteenth-century cloisonné enamels to a greater or less extent, although the split wires are often hidden by gilding. The bowl is decorated on the outside with Buddhist lions and brocade balls against a scroll background containing numerous emblems (Pl. 31B). The lotus petal border round the base, also a feature of the deep bowl, and the triangular border round the mouth-rim, are to be found in porcelain of the Chêng-tê period (1506–21). Inside the bowl there are galloping horses over waves and a four-pronged *vajra* on the base. The mark *Ta Ming nien tsao* is in cloisonné on the base beneath. The enamels are in great variety. There are eleven different colours, including the composite green-yellow as well as the 'Ming pink' formed from fragments of red and white. The bowl belongs to the first half of the century and probably to the first quarter. Other bowls in this group are decorated with the eight Buddhist emblems, the 'three friends' (pine, bamboo and plum), as well as simple lotus scrolls. The use of Buddhist emblems, and particularly the *vajra*, suggests that some of these bowls were made for temple use. But there is no doubt that Buddhist and Taoist emblems

THE SIXTEENTH CENTURY

were often used in the sixteenth century as mere objects of decoration. Many pieces in the Chia-ching lists of porcelain made for imperial use contain such emblems.[3]

The most common objects in this group are bowls and dishes, but there are vases, jars and incense burners as well. The leys jar (*cha-tou*) (Pl. 41A) has similar enamels to those on the bowl (Pl. 31B). It has Buddhist lions on the outside of the spreading mouth and galloping horses inside. The globular part has lotus scrolls with various emblems scattered over the scroll background. The shape of the vessel is close to that of blue and white enamelled leys jars of the Chêng-tê and early Chia-ching periods.[4]

A bowl of particular interest in this group is decorated on the outside with dragons in clouds and inside with fishes in waves surrounded by a lotus scroll border (Pl. 31A). The border of lotus petals round the base, the narrower borders round the foot and mouth rims and the scrolls filling in the background all point to a sixteenth-century date, as does the more advanced enamel palette. On the other hand, the dragon closely resembles a type which was used a good deal in late fifteenth-century porcelain and has come to be accepted as an indication of late fifteenth-century date. The characteristics are a snout in the form of an elephant's trunk, two front feet with claws, small wings and an elaborate foliated tail. The porcelain examples in addition often have a flowering lotus stem emerging from the mouth of the dragon. Such a dragon is to be found, for example, on a blue and white bowl at Ardebil.[5] This bowl has a four-pronged *vajra* inside, a further point of association with the group of cloisonné bowls. Other porcelain pieces have this type of dragon with what is interpreted as a string of pearls emerging from the mouth in place of the lotus branch.

There can be no doubt that many of the porcelain vases and bowls with this type of dragon are attributable, on reasonably good grounds, to the latter part of the fifteenth century. On this basis the cloisonné bowl was ascribed to the late fifteenth century in the Ming Exhibition of the Oriental Ceramic Society in 1957.[6] But since then reasons to doubt this attribution have come forward. The types of enamel, the scroll background and other details of the decoration all point to a date in the first half of the sixteenth century, possibly the first quarter. At least three other pieces in cloisonné with this type of dragon are known. Two of them have dragons with both a lotus stem and a string of pearls issuing from the mouth. The first is an ewer, formerly in the Kitson Collection, which has been extensively reconstructed (Pl. 33) and the second a vase with the Ching-t'ai mark in the British Museum which has had new mounts added in the seventeenth or

---

[3] S. W. Bushell, *Description of Chinese pottery and porcelain, being a translation of the T'ao Shuo*, 1910.
[4] Soame Jenyns, *Ming pottery and porcelain*, 1953, Pls. 84A, 85.
[5] John A. Pope, *Chinese porcelains from the Ardebil shrine*, p. 110, Pl. 62.
[6] *The arts of the Ming dynasty*, 1958, p. 50.

THE SIXTEENTH CENTURY

eighteenth century. In all three pieces the enamels and style of decoration suggest a sixteenth rather than a fifteenth century date.

At the entrance to the valley of the thirteen Ming tombs north of Peking there is a five-fold white marble entrance gate (*p'ai-lou*).[7, 8, 9] This fine structure is carved entirely from solid natural stone. The six pillars are supported on massive square pedestals carved with Buddhist lions and dragons. The decoration of the two outside pedestals is of Buddhist lions playing with brocade balls. The inner four pedestals are decorated with dragons, the two central ones with five-clawed dragons in the usual imperial form (Pl. 32A)[10] and the outer ones with dragons of the type already mentioned as associated with porcelain pieces of the late fifteenth century. These dragons have elephant snouts, two front feet, foliated tails and a flowering lotus stem emerging from the mouth (Pl. 32B).[10] The two feet have four, and not five, claws as would be expected in the dragons decorating an imperial entrance. The date of construction of the *p'ai-lou* is said to be 1540, but it is not known whether this date is based on firm evidence or not. Moreover it seems possible that the pedestals were made for some other purpose originally and were afterwards converted for use with the *p'ai-lou*. No documentary evidence is known to support this tentative suggestion but it would seem that the decoration of the panels terminates abruptly at the bases, which are roughly broken off in a manner which would hardly occur in the normal erection of the *p'ai-lou*. Moreover, the whole of the *p'ai-lou* is made of white marble except for the pedestals, which are described by de Groot[11] as made of a 'deep-blue kind of stone, nicely polished and very hard and durable'.

Stylistically the five-clawed dragons appear to be earlier than the date which has been given for the erection of the *p'ai-lou*. But the most important point seems to be the association of the foliated dragon with the conventional dragon. This suggests that the foliated dragon has a special significance, possibly Buddhist in origin, which has no connection with a particular period.[12] The arguments that have been put forward to connect this type of dragon with the Ch'êng-hua period are not, in the light of this evidence, very convincing. As far as the cloisonné pieces with this dragon are concerned, the internal evidence supporting an early sixteenth-century date is far stronger than the evidence, formerly accepted, which would have placed them in the late fifteenth century.

[7] C. Imbault-Huart, 'Les tombeaux des Ming près de Peking', *T'oung Pao*, Vol. IV, 1893.
[8] J. J. M. de Groot, *The religious system of China*, Vol. III, 1897.
[9] G. Bouillard, *Peking et ses environs, IIIe Series, Les tombeaux imperiaux des dynasties Ming et Ts'ing*, 1922.
[10] I am indebted to Mr. John Addis for the photographs of the pedestals and for much useful information about the *p'ai-lou*. [11] Reference 8.
[12] There does not seem to be any close connection between these dragons and the *ch'ih*, the child-dragon with foliated tail, that occurs so frequently in seventeenth-century designs. See Schuyler Cammann, 'Some strange Ming beasts', *Oriental Art*, Vol. II, No. 3, new series, 1956.

THE SIXTEENTH CENTURY

Another well defined sixteenth-century group consists of dishes whose main feature is a central subject on a ground of one colour surrounded by a floral border on a ground of different colour.[13] The dish with grape vines as its main subject (Pl. 34) is typical of the group. The grape vines, making use of the semi-translucent purple for the grapes and a composite yellow and green enamel shading to red for the leaves, are on a white ground, while the floral border is on a turquoise-blue ground. This dish was for a long time regarded as belonging to the fifteenth,[14] or even to the fourteenth,[15] century, but the most likely date of its manufacture is the first half, and probably the first quarter, of the sixteenth century. The dishes are made of cast bronze, and not of sheet copper, the usual material for sixteenth-century dishes and bowls, and the whole of the underside is nearly always plain metal.[16] The dishes generally have a hole in the centre, which has been carefully filled in, and most of them have had three small cloud-scroll feet fitted. It is likely that the dishes were originally the bases of simple pricket candlesticks and have been converted to dishes or salvers. No complete pricket candlestick of this type is known to the author. Two other examples of these dishes are shown in Plates 35 and 36. The former, a particularly attractive dish decorated with fruiting sprays, has a ground colour of an unusually deep turquoise-blue, while the floral border is on a ground formed of the composite yellow-green enamel. The other has cranes and water plants on a dark-green background, with a floral border of yellow flowers on a turquoise-blue ground. Another dish, with a much narrower flanged rim, is decorated with two mandarin ducks swimming on a lotus pond (Pl. 37). Like the rest, this dish has a bronze base and the usual tell-tale hole through the centre.

The small box, with no foot-rim and decorated all over with grape vines on the top and flowers on the bottom (Pls. 40A, B), has close affinities with the group of dishes. The ground colours are white for the grape vines (the usual background for this subject) and turquoise-blue for the flowers. The use of two different subjects for the top and bottom halves of boxes is fairly common in carved lacquer belonging to the first half of the sixteenth century.

Another piece with close affinities to the group of dishes is the attractive box with the unusual decoration on the top of two parrots perched on a spray of fruiting peaches (Col. Pl. E). This was at one time thought to be one of the earliest pieces of Ming cloisonné,[17] but a

---

[13] No fifteenth-century example known to the author has a ground colour other than turquoise-blue, except the large dragon jar in the British Museum (Pl. 12), in which the background, of clouds, is in many colours.

[14] *Catalogue of International Exhibition of Chinese Art*, 1935–6, No. 2024.

[15] H. C. Gallois, 'About T'ang and Ta Ts'in', *O.C.S. Transactions*, Vol. 13, 1935–6.

[16] Two pieces in this group are true dishes with cloisonné decoration on the edge beneath and plain bronze bases. One belongs to Mr. G. de Menasce (*Arts of the Ming dynasty*, No. 230, Pl. 84) and the other is in the Royal Scottish Museum.

[17] Soame Jenyns, 'The problems of Chinese cloisonné enamels', *O.C.S. Transactions*, Vol. 25, p. 63, 1949–50.

E. EARLY SIXTEENTH CENTURY. DIAMETER 10·0 in.
British Museum
See pp. 72–3

THE SIXTEENTH CENTURY

comparison of the enamel colours alone with those of the dish in Colour Plate B is sufficient to show that the box is much later. In particular the semi-translucent brown, used effectively for the stems of the peach sprays in the box, is one that never occurs in fifteenth-century work. The cobalt-blue, used sparingly, is almost greyish black. The open design has led to the filling in of the background with scroll work, which is applied with some skill. The box probably belongs to the first quarter of the sixteenth century.

All the pieces considered up to the present belong to the first half of the sixteenth century, and most of them to the first quarter, although the types may have persisted a little longer. They are therefore earlier than the few pieces known with the mark of Chia-ching, which have good claims to belong to the period. The sixteenth century has little to help us in the way of marks, which play such an important part in the dating of the porcelain of the century. All that we have, for the whole century, are four or five pieces with the mark of Chia-ching (1522–66) and about the same number with that of Wan-li (1573–1619). The Chia-ching marks are all incised and cannot therefore with complete certainty be regarded as contemporary. But the style of decoration, the enamels and the calligraphy of the marks provide such strong supporting evidence that the period may be accepted with confidence. The first of the pieces which we shall consider is a dish decorated with five-clawed dragons. This is of special importance because the design on the front of the dish is close to that of a well known group of blue and white dishes of the Chêng-tê and Chia-ching periods. The cloisonné dish, saucer-shaped, has a central panel with a five-clawed dragon amid lotus scrolls surrounded by a border of three dragons on a similar ground (Pl. 38A). The decoration round the rim underneath is unconventional, with six *ch'i-lin* against a background of rocks, fungus and bamboo (Pl. 38B). The mark is incised on the plain bronze base. The enamels are in simple plain colours, except for the addition of the mixed red and white enamel. The cobalt-blue is greyish.

The fifth claw of each foot of all the dragons has been mutilated in an attempt to erase it. The removal of the fifth claw is not uncommon in lacquer and porcelain of the Chia-ching period, particularly lacquer, and is generally thought to have been done to pieces stolen from the imperial collection. But the subject of the decoration on the underneath of the dish makes it doubtful whether this cloisonné dish was made for palace use.

The subsidiary scroll-work in the background of the dish is poor in quality and entirely unrelated to the main design. This effect is even more noticeable in the second marked piece, a bowl with an everted lip carrying the six-character Chia-ching mark incised on the base. The bowl is decorated, inside and out, with cranes flying through clouds (Pl. 39B). The colour scheme is simple with red, yellow, white, dark green and greyish cobalt-blue used for the cranes and clouds against a pale turquoise-blue ground. A similarly decorated piece, unmarked, is the sturdy pear-shaped vase (Pl. 39A). Here the background, of flower scrolls, is much better rendered, although far removed in design and finish from fifteenth-century work.

We saw that, in the fifteenth century, the shapes of the incense burners, in two forms, the *ting* and the *kuei*, conformed strictly to particular shapes. The shapes of the sixteenth-century incense burners show considerable changes. The type of *ting* as shown in Plates 17A and 19A was superseded by one in which the feet had become shorter and the side-handles were replaced by loop-handles forming an integral part of the plain mouth-rim (Pl. 40c). This shape is one of the most common in sixteenth-century wares, but many pieces have had the simple rims removed and replaced by more elaborate cast rims and handles in the seventeenth and eighteenth centuries. Finely perforated covers are often added as well. No sixteenth century incense burner of this kind is known to the author with an original cover. The *kuei* also showed changes in the sixteenth century although, as we have seen, the early shape survived for a short time (Pl. 30A). One of the new forms is that of the charming little piece decorated with birds on branches of pine, bamboo and plum (the 'three friends') (Pl. 41c). This bears an incised Ching-t'ai mark, but cannot be earlier than the sixteenth century.

There are a number of sixteenth-century pieces with shapes which can be closely matched by examples in porcelain and other materials. The ewer (Pl. 42), of slender flattened pear-shape with domed lid and heart-shaped panels on the body, is of a form that first appeared in blue and white porcelain during the Chêng-tê period, to be followed by many examples in the Chia-ching period, decorated in blue and white, red and green enamels and in the turquoise-blue and purple enamels of the *fa hua* group. There has been much discussion on the origin of this shape, which had been assumed for a long time to be Persian. But Basil Gray has pointed out[18] that there is no evidence to support a Persian origin. There can be no doubt that the porcelain ewers were derived from metal prototypes, for some of these ewers, and indeed the earlier ewers of the fifteenth century, often have strap-work with representations of rivets. The particular shape of ewer that concerns us, with heart-shaped raised panels, as we have said, does not seem to occur before the Chêng-tê period.[19] The gold ewer from the Eumorfopoulos Collection, formerly attributed to the Hsüan-tê period, probably belongs to the same period.[20]

The cloisonné ewer is decorated in a great variety of enamels, including the mixed colours yellow and green, yellow and red, as well as yellow, red and green. The background to the heart-shaped panels, each decorated with a *Ch'i-lin* in a landscape, is turquoise-blue and to

---

[18] Basil Gray, 'The influence of near eastern metalwork on Chinese ceramics', *O.C.S. Transactions*, 1941–2.   [19] Soame Jenyns, Reference 4, Pl. 54B.
[20] Sotheby & Co., Catalogue of the Eumorfopoulos Collection, May, 1940.

THE SIXTEENTH CENTURY

the surrounding floral scrolls a pulsating lapis-lazuli blue, as near an approach to the Mohammedan blue of the fifteenth century as we ever get in the sixteenth. The evidence provided by the enamels is consistent with that from the shape and makes a mid-sixteenth-century date very probable. Another ewer of similar shape, in the Victoria and Albert Museum, decorated with the eight Buddhist emblems amid lotus scrolls, is probably a little earlier. The faceted vase (Pl. 44B) resembles more closely the twelfth-century Persian bronze bottles from which it was undoubtedly derived[21] than do the well-known porcelain examples. Many of these bear the Hsüan-tê mark, but there are considerable differences of opinion as to whether any of them are as early as this.[22] The cloisonné vase, from the style of decoration and the enamels, almost certainly belongs to the first half of the sixteenth century. The handles are probably not the original ones.

Another shape found in cloisonné of the sixteenth century, although not, apparently, earlier, is the *mei p'ing*, a shape found in porcelain from late Sung and Yüan times. The *mei p'ing* decorated with mallows and lotus plants (Pl.44A) has a shape that does not conform exactly to any ceramic example. The bottle-shaped vase with masks and ring-handles (Pl. 43) is also unlike any sixteenth-century ceramic shape. No doubt the heavy bronze foot and mouth rims, appropriate for a metal piece, are responsible for the divergence. The *mei p'ing*, which has an added base containing a cast Ching-t'ai mark, belongs to the first half of the sixteenth century, while the bottle is a little later. The enamels of the latter, although they belong to a well-known group, are rather more translucent than usual.

Another piece of special interest is the jardinière or incense burner (Pl. 45) fitted with finely cast gilt-bronze handles in the form of lions standing on lions' heads and with claw feet, decorated in a great variety of enamels. The subject of decoration, a landscape, with some figures on the side not shown in the illustration, is handled in an unusually bold manner. The piece bears the Ching-t'ai mark cast in the base, but it cannot be earlier than the second half of the sixteenth century and it may indeed be later than this. A second piece, similar in shape and with almost identical gilt-bronze mounts, but fitted with a perforated cover and almost certainly intended for use as an incense burner, was shown in the Ming Exhibition of the Oriental Ceramic Society in 1957.[23] It has the engraved mark of Hsüan-tê on the base, but while the enamel decoration of lotus scrolls is undoubtedly earlier than that on the former piece it is far removed from fifteenth-century work. The most likely date of manufacture is the second quarter of the sixteenth century.

Reference has been made to the small group of pieces with the Wan-li mark. They all have the mark *Ta Ming Wan-li nien tsao* in cloisonné enamel on the base. They are of outstanding documentary

[21] Reference 18, Pl. 6. [22] Reference 4, Pls. 51A, 51B.
[23] Reference 6, No. 318, Pl. 85.

THE SIXTEENTH CENTURY

importance as the only pieces with contemporary marks of the sixteenth century that can be accepted without question as belonging to the period of the mark. Nearly all the pieces in the group are large dishes with flanged rims in many foliations and decorated with five-clawed dragons in clouds surrounded by floral borders (Col. Pl. F). A similar dish to this one, belonging to the British Museum, is to be seen in the Victoria and Albert Museum while a rather different one in the Chinese Imperial Collection, now at Taiwan, was exhibited in the International Exhibition of Chinese Art in 1935.[24] The small cylindrical box (Pl. 47A), decorated on the top with a *shou* character surrounded by leaf scrolls and on the sides with flower sprays and bamboo leaves, belongs to the same group. The background colour to all these pieces is a pale turquoise-blue and the other enamels include some mixed colours, one of which is the composite yellow and red. The marks on the dish and the box are shown in Plates 47c and 47B.

To the second half of the sixteenth century belong a series of deep dishes with flat bases and wide flanged rims decorated with a wide variety of subjects. Some of these dishes are of poor quality, with thin layers of enamel, so that the colour of the base metal shows through, but the best are extremely decorative, with a great variety of colours including some mixed enamels not found earlier. Some of the dishes are on bases of copper sheet, and these are enamelled over the whole of the underneath, including the flat base, which has no foot-rim. Others are of bronze and are enamelled only on the front. The latter, curiously enough, are generally the finer in quality. The poorer dishes have often been confused with Japanese nineteenth-century cloisonné, but there is no excuse for the confusion, because in the Ming dishes the wires are secured by solder, which is particularly evident when, as is usually the case, the piece has suffered damage. However badly the the piece may be damaged the wires will always be found to be securely attached. The later Japanese pieces have no solder and if they are severely damaged the wires, as well as the enamels, will often be found to have broken away.

The subjects of decoration of these dishes include many not to be found in the earlier sixteenth-century cloisonné. For the first time we find elaborate landscapes with a great variety of plants, animals and birds as well as human figures in garden scenes. It is a curious fact that cloisonné with human figures does not seem to occur until the second half of the sixteenth century, although figural scenes are to be found in porcelain and lacquer, particularly the latter, from the early fifteenth century onwards. Two dishes (Pls. 48, 49), both decorated with figures in a garden with pavilions, show the type at its best. They are each on a bronze base, undecorated beneath. A feature in the decoration in these dishes is the diamond or lozenge pattern border on the flange, with a simple floral border on the outside and a fret border inside.

[24] No. 2005, illustrated in Pl. 6 of the *Catalogue of Chinese Government Exhibits*, Vol. IV.

F. WAN-LI MARK AND PERIOD.   DIAMETER 19·7 in.
British Museum
See pp. 76, 109

THE SIXTEENTH CENTURY

This type of border seems peculiar to cloisonné and may indicate a particular factory.

Other dishes in this group have as their central theme landscapes with birds and animals, similar to the subjects to be found in the so-called export porcelain of the late sixteenth and early seventeenth centuries. It is tempting to use the term 'export type' to describe the cloisonné dishes, but there is no evidence to support the view that they were exported more often than the other types.

Towards the end of the sixteeenth century the large so-called 'temple vessels' began to be made in large numbers. Most of these have the finely divided mixed enamels and they seem to have been made right up to the end of the Ming dynasty and even into the early years of the Ch'ing. It is convenient to deal with them in the next chapter, on the Transitional wares, but it must not be thought that there is any clear demarcation between the late wares of the sixteenth century and the early ones of the seventeenth.

8. The Transitional Period

The decline of the Ming dynasty had set in before the death of the last great Ming emperor, Wan-li, in 1619. During the later years of his reign the government of the country became more and more corrupt. Greatly increased taxation and the creation of large estates for court favourites, as a result of which large numbers of peasants were expelled from their farms, had caused civil war to break out in many parts of the country by the end of the reign. The Manchus in the north were able to take advantage of these internal dissensions. They gradually over-ran the whole of the country and set up a new dynasty in 1644. The new regime, however, was not firmly established and continual attempts to re-establish the native Ming dynasty went on for many years. Even after 1659, when the last Ming prince was killed in Yunnan, spasmodic insurrections continued. The last was in 1674, when Wu San-kuei, the viceroy of Yunnan, invaded and occupied the province of Kiangsi. During these operations the imperial porcelain factory at Ching-tê Chên was totally destroyed. But by 1681 the rebellion was finally suppressed and China entered a peaceful and prosperous era under the wise guidance of the Emperor K'ang-hsi, who had ascended the throne as a child in 1662.

One result of the breakdown that followed the death of Wan-li was that the official patronage of the arts and crafts almost disappeared. While large amounts of porcelain, lacquer and textiles, as well as work in many other materials, had been produced for the Wan-li court we find that little corresponding material was made for the later Ming emperors. We might at first sight imagine that the lack of official support would have had a disastrous effect on the arts and crafts. In fact the reverse happened. The release of the craftsmen from official control allowed the impact of new ideas to make itself felt and the seventeenth century saw an awakening of inspiration in all the applied arts.

The major art of painting did not, like the minor arts, come under close official patronage at any time during the Ming dynasty. The collapse of the dynasty did not therefore affect the activities of the scholar painters, except to cause some of them to flee to remote parts of the country, and we find that landscape painting maintained a high level throughout the whole of this troubled period. The minor arts, with official restrictions removed, were able to benefit from the influence of the seventeenth-century painters. We find this influence most

THE TRANSITIONAL PERIOD

noticeable in the painting of porcelain. The old stereotyped designs, laid down in the official lists of Chia-ching, Lung-ch'ing and Wan-li, were abandoned, to be replaced by naturalistic representations of flowers and rocks, mountain landscapes, and garden scenes and landscapes with human figures. The shapes of the vases, while not particularly distinguished, are truly ceramic, the ugly bronze shapes of the Wan-li period being completely discarded. On these simple shapes the painters delineated their flowers and landscapes with great skill, sometimes in a purely linear style and at other times using graded washes which eventually led to the most characteristic work of the K'ang-hsi period.

What is really surprising about the porcelain of this period, and this point has not been stressed sufficiently by writers on the subject, is its high intrinsic quality. The materials of the body and glaze of the best of these pieces are as fine as those of any imperial Chia-ching or Wan-li wares, while the quality of the underglaze blue, in the blue and white, is superior, in many eyes, to all but the very best of the sixteenth-century wares. The implication of this must be that, in spite of the removal of official orders, the standard of manufacture of the best porcelain at Ching-tê Chên was maintained, and even raised, during most of this period. It is difficult to explain why, in relation to this excellence of material, the few pieces bearing an official *nien hao* are so poor in quality. The few pieces known today with the reign marks of the last two Ming emperors, T'ien-ch'i (1621–7) and Ch'ung-chêng (1628–43) are roughly finished, the materials of body and glaze are coarse and the blue in the underglaze blue and white are as poor as anything to be found in the Ming dynasty.

The lack of appreciation of the non-imperial wares of the seventeenth century in the West, which still persists, in spite of the enthusiasm of a small group of collectors, must be attributed to the fact that the pieces, bearing no mark, cannot be grouped and precisely labelled as can, for example, the porcelain of the sixteenth century. We cannot even be certain at times whether a piece should be called Ming or Ch'ing. This uncertainty is a great disadvantage in the eyes of those collectors who desire, above all, to be able to give a precise attribution to their pieces.

A study of the other arts of the period, such as lacquer and cloisonné, reveals the same general qualities as we have described in porcelain. In spite of the disturbed political conditions, the standards of manufacture showed no decline while at the same time new inspiration replaced the outworn formulae of the official regulations. As a result, we find in all these materials new and important advances, many of which have been accredited to the K'ang-hsi period, whereas, in fact, this period was often only responsible for the refinement of techniques and ideas first developed in the middle years of the century.

The term 'Transitional Period' has been applied to this no-man's land, comprising broadly the sixty years following the death of

THE TRANSITIONAL PERIOD

Wan-li, by students and connoisseurs of porcelain, because they have seen in it the development of new types of porcelain which led to the wares of the Ch'ing dynasty.[1] In one sense the term is a good one. But it does less than justice to a period in which there were introduced many new ideas and techniques, and it deserves to stand on its own feet, rather than be described by this rather nebulous term. However, the term is now well established for porcelain and since the pattern for development in cloisonné and other materials resembles that followed by porcelain the term 'Transitional Period' is a satisfactory one for general use.

The seventeenth century saw some important, even revolutionary, changes in the methods of manufacture of cloisonné. These have already been fully discussed in Chapter 4. They include the introduction of wire-drawing methods for the manufacture of the wires, the change in the material of the wire from bronze to copper and the gradual abandonment of the use of solder as a means of fixing the wire to the base. These changes took a long time to come into effect and it is likely that their introduction was more rapid in some factories than in others, so that it is difficult to use the presence or absence of a particular feature as a means of precise, rather than approximate, dating. We know that by the end of the century the change-over to copper wire, produced in uniform thicknesses by wire-drawing methods, was virtually complete. It is likely that the setting up of the imperial factory in Peking round about 1680, which we shall discuss in the next chapter, had the effect of standardizing the methods of production. The improvement in technical processes that took place during the century led eventually to methods of mass production which destroyed much of the individuality of the earlier work. But the effects of these new processes were not fully felt until the end of the century and much seventeenth-century work shows an individuality and freshness that makes it very attractive.

The enamels of the seventeenth century do not at first show very much change over those of the sixteenth, except for the tendency of the mixed enamels to be more finely divided. In particular a yellow-green derived from a green enamel paste with fine specks of yellow appeared for the first time and was used very widely. The same wide range of colours as was developed in the sixteenth century was used, and even extended, with great decorative effect. At the end of the seventeenth century new colours, some of them not particularly attractive, began to appear, but these call more properly to be dealt with in the next chapter, as does the rose-pink enamel derived from gold. This enamel is never found in cloisonné of the seventeenth century.

We can get no help in dating pieces of seventeenth-century cloisonné from marks. Not a single seventeenth-century reign mark on cloisonné

---

[1] The best description of this period, with special reference to porcelain, is that of Soame Jenyns, 'The wares of the transitional period between the Ming and the Ch'ing, 1620–1683, *Archives of the Chinese Art Society of America*, Vol. IX, 1955.

THE TRANSITIONAL PERIOD

belonging to the transitional period is known and the only marks to be found at all are those of the Ching-t'ai period. Many of these have been added at some time in the Ch'ing dynasty but there are a few pieces, probably belonging to the middle of the century or later, with Ching-t'ai marks which may be contemporary with the piece.

We are left therefore with no means of determining the dates of manufacture except by a study of the stylistic qualities of the designs, the enamels and the techniques adopted in manufacture. Although there is, as we have said, a great difference between the cloisonné made in the first quarter of the century and that made in the last, the intermediate period is difficult, as indeed it is in porcelain. Nevertheless there are distinctive features which can be used to give us some guidance.

One of the most important groups of cloisonné of the seventeenth century consists of large vases and similar objects made for the decoration of Buddhist temples. The temple vessels derive from earlier smaller incense burners and vases of the fifteenth and sixteenth centuries, but by the early seventeenth century, or even a little earlier, they had become larger and more imposing. Many of them were made in sets for the decoration of altars, generally comprising a large central incense burner, flanked by two pricket candlesticks and two flower vases. Few complete sets survive today, but there are three large pieces of a set, consisting of two pricket candlesticks and a flower vase, in enamelled porcelain, each with the Wan-li mark, in the British Museum.[2] The decoration of the cloisonné vessels is provided by lotus scrolls (Pl. 50, 51 A) or archaistic designs derived from ancient bronzes. A beaker (*ku*) with this latter type of decoration (Pl. 52) bears the Ching-t'ai mark cast in the base which, as we so often find, has been made separately and soldered on with great skill. The use of copper for the addition shows that the foot was added in the eighteenth century. The shapes of these vessels are almost always based on those of ancient bronzes, such as the *ku*, *hu* and *ting*. The vessels are well made and the enamels cover a wide range of colours, generally set against a deep turquoise-blue ground.

Other large vessels belonging to this group are decorated in a less formal manner with landscapes of trees, flowering plants and rocks providing the background for a great variety of animals, birds and insects. The colours of the enamels are brilliant and the use of mixed colours to give new effects is exploited to the limit. The large four-sided jar (Pl. 53), for instance, has one mixed colour with four components, dark green, light green, red and yellow. There is another with red, white and blue used to provide an unusual pale lilac. Some larger dishes with dragons and phoenixes also belong to this group. One of these was exhibited in the O.C.S. Ming Exhibition in 1957.[3] Another

[2] R. L. Hobson, *Handbook of the pottery and porcelain of the Far East*, 1948, Pl. XII, Fig. 100; *British Museum Quarterly*, Vol. V, No. 3, 1930, Pls. XXXIX, XL.
[3] *The arts of the Ming dynasty*, 1958, No. 315.

(Pl. 60), although it has some resemblance to the Wan-li dish with two dragons in the British Museum (Col. Pl. D), is certainly, from the types of enamels and the style of the dragon, of later date, probably made near the middle of the century. A smaller dish with six simply rendered archaic dragons surrounded by lotus scrolls (Pl. 51B) belongs to about the same period. The same design of dragons appears in a roundel on a piece of seventeenth-century k'o-ssŭ in the Victoria and Albert Museum.

Among the most brilliant of the cloisonné wares of the seventeenth century are some large panels decorated with landscapes. These panels seem to have been made for insertion into pieces of furniture and not, as were similar panels of the eighteenth century, intended to be framed as pictures. The colours of these early panels are in great variety, many shades of blue and green, for example, being used to delineate mountains. For sheer brilliance there is nothing else in Chinese cloisonné that quite approaches them. The best eighteenth-century panels, charming as they are (Pl. 77), look rather subdued when placed side by side with the vigorous seventeenth-century examples. Many of the panels have borders of archaistic dragons resembling those to be found in porcelain and lacquer of the T'ien-ch'i period. The one chosen for illustration here has a simpler border of flower or fungus scrolls (Pl. 56). The landscape scene represents the Worthies of the Orchid Pavilion floating their wine-cups down the 'nine-bend river',[4] a popular subject in the decoration of blue and white porcelain of the seventeenth century. This celebrated group of literati and wine-bibbers, who lived in the fourth century, are described by the T'ang poet Tu Fu.

The unusual arm rest, in the form of a scroll, decorated with figures in a garden (Pl. 57), may, from the similarity of the enamels to those of the pieces just described, be attributed to about the same period. It belongs to a small group with the peculiarity that the faces of the figures are left blank, with no wire details. Since the standard of workmanship of these pieces is very high, it seems unlikely that the faces were left without details in the first place and it may be that they were decorated either by gilding or painting, which has worn off. In the arm rest the faces of the three principal figures are made of mother-of-pearl insets with incised features. These may well have been added later.

Another group of pieces, probably belonging to about the middle of the century, has the turquoise-blue background in an unusual greenish tinge. The decoration is usually of freely drawn flowers, plants and rocks. The attractive moon vase, decorated with carnations, an unusual subject, on one side (Pl. 54) and peonies on the other, is a typical example, as are the two small panels, one with fruiting vines (Pl. 55A) and the other with melons (Pl. 55B).

Ming figures of animals and birds are rare, and they almost all belong to the seventeenth century. There may be one or two as early as

[4] R. L. Hobson, *The later ceramic wares of China*, 1925.

THE TRANSITIONAL PERIOD

the end of the sixteenth century, such as the attractive deer in unusual colours, mostly of brown and yellow (Pl. 58B). A number of figures of ducks are known, generally mounted on square or rhomboidal bases, decorated in enamels different from those of the ducks themselves. The enamels of the figures and bases, however, appear to be contemporary and it seems likely that, in spite of a little incongruity in the pieces, they were made in their present form. The duck in Plate 58A is complete in itself. It is decorated in a finely divided composite green-yellow, white, turquoise-blue, cobalt-blue and the semi-translucent purple which is a feature of so many Ming pieces. This enamel does not seem to occur in the following dynasty. The well-modelled figure of a magpie (Pl. 59) may well be a little later, although it has good claims to belong to the seventeenth century.

Mention has already been made, in Chapter 6, of a group of pieces bearing the Ching-t'ai mark in enamel. The characteristics of the group are the use of bronze wires of even thickness, with little or no soldering, and enamels of Ming type, including some mixed colours. The turquoise-blue that forms the base colour is paler and more greenish than usual. A feature of all the pieces is that the first application of enamel over the whole piece is turquoise-blue, the other colours being placed on this ground colour for a second and subsequent firings. The box of Plate 61D is a typical example. The four-character mark on the base is in a square panel of cloisonné surrounded by simple flower sprays. The mark is shown in Plate 61E. The dating of this group is not an easy problem, but the most likely date of manufacture is the end of the transitional period. We cannot rule out, however, a somewhat later date.

An interesting group of *ju-i* sceptres, although certainly belonging to the seventeenth century, presents some difficulty in precise dating. The shape is best known from the many eighteenth-century examples in jade, lacquer, cloisonné, porcelain and other materials. These sceptres were given as birthday presents and are often inscribed with wishes for long life and prosperity.[5] The term '*ju-i* head' has been applied to the head of the sceptre, which is generally in a form (Pl. 61A) similar to one used in decorative borders on porcelain. Cammann[6] has associated this design with that of the collars of dragon robes known as *yun chien*, 'cloud collars', and we may note that the conventional treatment of clouds in porcelain, lacquer and textiles in the fifteenth and sixteenth centuries closely follow the '*ju-i* head' form.

The early history of the *ju-i* is obscure. The earliest reference to it occurs in a biography of Hu Tsung, a statesman who died in A.D. 243. Laufer[7] agrees with Giles[8] in following the thirteenth-century book,

[5] The literal meaning of *ju-i* is 'as desired'. In modern Chinese and Japanese dictionaries the term is defined as a backscratcher, principally because of the shape.

[6] Schuyler Cammann, 'The symbolism of the cloud collar', *The Art Bulletin*, Vol. 33, March, 1951.

[7] Berthold Laufer, *Jade, a study of Chinese archaeology and religion*, 1912.

[8] Herbert A. Giles, *History of Chinese pictorial art*, 1905.

THE TRANSITIONAL PERIOD

the *Tung t'ien ch'ung lu*, which says, 'The men of old used the *ju-i* for pointing the way and also for guarding against the unforeseen. It was made of wrought iron and was over two feet in length, ornamented with patterns of silver, either inlaid or overlaid.' Laufer also associates the *ju-i* with the Bodhisattva Mañjuśrī (Wên Shu), who sometimes holds the sceptre instead of the more usual sword. In the Freer Gallery of Art there is a Buddhist stele dated A.D. 564 on which is depicted the meeting of Mañjuśrī with the devout layman Vimalakīrti (Wei-mo-chi).[9] Mañjuśrī is carrying a *ju-i* and Davidson establishes the point that the *ju-i* is a symbol of debate. Up to the tenth century it was associated only with Mañjuśrī but afterwards it was a common attribute of teachers and preachers, who carried the *ju-i* as a symbol of authority in debate. A number of *ju-i* which date from the eighth century are preserved in the Shōsō-in. They are simple tapered metal rods or strips bent over at the end.[10]

At times the *ju-i* was made to represent natural branches and there are two bronze *ju-i* in the Shōsō-in simulating bamboo. The later developments of the *ju-i*, after the decline of Buddhism, are difficult to follow, but it seems to have associations with the flowering branch of the lotus carried by certain Bodhisattvas, especially Kuan-yin, the 'lotus bearer'. The title goes back to the Sanskrit *Padmapani*. Giles refers to a painting dated 1508 with a goddess and attendant, in which the latter is carrying a *ju-i*, and there are known a number of Ming figures carrying objects, not always easily identifiable, varying from a lotus flower on the one hand to a formal sceptre on the other.

The earliest dated sceptre known to the author is in the Royal Ontario Museum of Archaeology, Toronto. It is of iron, nearly two feet in length, inlaid with inscriptions in silver and dated 1622.[11] The head is of quatrefoil and not the usual *ju-i* shape and the stem consists of a parallel section joined to the head by a narrow strip. The inscription records that the sceptre was a present to Chao Nan-hsing, a known dignitary of the Wan-li period. It is worthy of note that this sceptre, in its material, method of decoration and even in size follows closely the one described in the thirteenth-century *Tung t'ien ch'ung lu*.

The cloisonné sceptres that concern us (Pls. 61A, B, C) are decorated in enamels of typical Ming types. The turquoise-blue background is greenish and the other enamels are a greyish cobalt-blue, dark green, a composite yellow-green, red, yellow, white and the semi-translucent brown. The body is of cast bronze and the wires are also of bronze. The head, in true *ju-i* form, and the stem are made separately and afterwards soldered together. An interesting feature of the wire-work is that many of the components are of the same size. For example, in the tapered stem of the sceptre of Plate 61B, the bats are in two sizes, two being of one size and two of another. On the back of the stem (Pl. 61c)

[9] J. LeRoy Davidson, 'The origin and early use of the ju-i', *Artibus Asiae*, Vol. XIII, 1950. [10] Reference 9.
[11] *The arts of the Ming dynasty*, Detroit Institute of Arts, 1952, No. 321.

THE TRANSITIONAL PERIOD

there are nine lotus flowers and instead of the size of the flowers gradually diminishing as the stem narrows we find four of one size and five of another. This suggests that the outlines of the bats and lotus flowers were made separately of wire components soldered together and then inserted in the piece. In spite of this example of mass production, which might suggest a late date, all the other features of the sceptres point to a mid-seventeenth century date. The subjects of decoration of the sceptres, on the other hand, suggest a rather later date than this. The sceptre on Plate 61B is decorated with nine red bats, five on the head and four on the stem, and the characters *kao shou k'ang ning*, 'health and tranquillity in old age', are depicted on the stem, with various cloud and wave motives. In the centre of the head is the *Yin-yang* symbol. Now bats as a subject of decoration are rarely found before the Ch'ing dynasty. Moreover the use of red bats, *hung fu*, a homophone for 'vast happiness', the written characters being quite different, is one of the many punning allusions that were so popular in the Ch'ing dynasty. Some authorities think that the use of homophones in this way rarely occurred before the eighteenth century.

Thus we have the apparent conflict between the evidence that comes from the technical quality of the pieces and the subjects of decoration. Many sceptres of the eighteenth century, with rose-pink and other late enamels, more complex in shape than the sceptres considered here and with protuberances in the middle and at the lower end (Pl. 69B), belong to a different group. The weight of the evidence seems to the author to suggest that the more simple sceptres were made before the setting up of the imperial factory round about 1680 and that they are truly transitional wares. It is of interest to record that the sceptres in the past have generally been given a K'ang-hsi attribution.[12]

The last major group to be considered in this chapter also presents some difficulties, and it is not easy to determine whether the pieces were made before 1680, and therefore come into the transitional group, or whether they were made a little later. The pieces are remarkably consistent in design, decoration and enamels. The enamel range is limited to a dark greyish cobalt-blue, red, yellow, white and the semi-translucent brown set against a turquoise-blue that is quite distinctive, having less green in it than the normal Ming colour. The decoration makes great use of archaistic dragons in cobalt-blue, often supplemented by good luck characters such as *shou*, 'long life', in red. The pieces themselves are generally small intimate pieces of distinctive shapes, with a decided preference for foliated sections. Typical examples are the pricket candlestick (Pl. 62A), the bowl-stand with six-foil edge (Pl. 62B) and the foliated box and cover (Pl. 63A). The annular box with hinged lid, no doubt intended for use as a container

---

[12] A sceptre similar to that of Plate 61B, in the Metropolitan Museum of Art, New York, has been given this attribution (*Encyclopaedia Britannica*, 1947, article on enamels).

THE TRANSITIONAL PERIOD

of necklaces (Pl. 63B), has dragon panels set in a brocade ground of a type that became very popular in the eighteenth century.

The consistency in the designs and the close conformity in the colours of the enamels suggest that the pieces were made in a single factory in which close control was maintained. Such a control was certainly in force in the imperial factory set up round about 1680 and one is tempted to think that the pieces were made in this factory. But the technical characteristics of the pieces themselves suggest an earlier date. The wires are of bronze, and although more uniform in thickness than those made at the beginning of the century, still show signs of hand craftsmanship. Furthermore the enamels are very close to those of the Ming dynasty. On the whole, the evidence is in favour of a date of manufacture just before 1680.

The tall cylindrical ewer, divided into four sections each with a spirited five-clawed dragon, surmounted by a deep flanged lip decorated with a fifth dragon, and with dragon handle and spout (Pl. 64), is of a shape found in porcelain and other materials. The inside of the flanged lip is decorated with galloping horses above waves in typical Ming style. A number of the porcelain ewers, fitted with bosses to take cords or chains instead of fixed handles, decorated in enamels on the biscuit in late Ming style, have generally been attributed to the early K'ang-hsi period. This seems to be the most likely date for the cloisonné example. Such ewers are often called 'distilling jars' and they may have been used for some simple distillation process.

The large stand (Pl. 65) also has Ming features in the decoration, and would stylistically be dated before 1680. But the complexity and size of this imposing piece imply manufacturing facilities such as could only be provided in a very large well-equipped factory. The stand may therefore belong to the first few years of the new factory, but we need to know more about the early history of this factory before problems such as this can be finally solved. Little is known at present about the early productions of any of the great imperial factories set up by K'ang-hsi round about 1680. In its impact on the Ch'ing arts and crafts this was probably the most important period in the whole of the dynasty and it is surprising that so little interest and study have been devoted to it.

9. The Ch'ing Dynasty

We have seen how the seventeenth century was a time in which new technological processes in the manufacture of cloisonné enamels were being introduced, and we know that new methods, all directed towards easy mass production, were well established by the first quarter of the eighteenth century. It is not easy to say at what stage during the last half of the seventeenth century the new techniques were introduced. It seems likely, however, that a turning point was reached when a new factory for the manufacture of cloisonné enamels was set up in Peking round about 1680.

The young emperor K'ang-hsi, who ascended the throne in 1662, when he was only eight years old, began to take an active part in the administration of the country even before he reached manhood. He took a great interest in improving the arts and crafts of his country and conceived the idea of setting up, within the precincts of the imperial palace in Peking, a number of workshops, each responsible for a particular craft. This involved the collection of skilled workmen from all over China and must have taken some years to put into effect. It is recorded that by 1680 some thirty factories in all had been set up by the Bureau of Works, the *Tsao-pan Ch'u*, in the Forbidden City.[1] These were made responsible for work in a great variety of crafts, one of which was the manufacture of cloisonné enamels.[2] The only great industry not represented was the manufacture of porcelain. Père d'Entrecolles, in his letter of 1st September, 1712,[3] tells us of attempts made by the emperor to set up porcelain kilns in Peking. Workmen and materials were sent from Ching-tê Chên, but in spite of great efforts the venture failed. Père d'Entrecolles conjectures that the scheme may have failed for political reasons, but it seems more likely that the reasons were economic. The large amounts of material, including fuel, needed for the manufacture of porcelain, and the high temperature needed for firing would have made it very difficult to set up a factory within the precincts of the palace. The manufacture of cloisonné, requiring relatively small amounts of material and a relatively low temperature of firing, was a much more manageable project.

[1] For a full account of the history of these workshops see Lady David, *Illustrated catalogue of Ch'ing enamelled porcelain in the Percival David Foundation*, 1958.

[2] S. W. Bushell, *Chinese Art*, 1914, Vol. I, p. 108, gives a full list of the crafts for which workshops were provided.

[3] S. W. Bushell, *A description of Chinese pottery and porcelain, being a translation of the T'ao Shuo*, 1910, p. 183.

THE CH'ING DYNASTY

The cloisonné factory was almost certainly used later on, towards the end of the reign of K'ang-hsi, for the enamelling of plain porcelain sent from Ching-tê Chên to Peking for decoration.

Soulié de Morant has suggested[4] that painted enamels were made in the cloisonné factory as early as 1683. The subject of painted enamels is outside the scope of this book, except for the study of a small group of pieces with both types of enamel in combination, but the date of introduction of painted enamels is of importance to us, because it determines the stage at which the rose-pink enamel derived from gold, the so-called *famille rose*, was introduced. This enamel played an important part in the decoration of the later cloisonné. There is no support today for the view that painted enamels were made as early as 1683. The evidence available suggests that they were not introduced into China before the last few years of K'ang-hsi.

The emperor seems to have taken a special interest in the manufacture of cloisonné vessels for use in Buddhist temples. It was his practice to present to these temples, at their inauguration, sets of ritual vessels. Bushell tells us that there were still to be seen, when he was in China at the beginning of the present century, fine specimens of cloisonné in the Buddhist temples near Peking.[5] The Emperor Yung-chêng, when he came to the throne in 1723, consecrated his former residence as the great Lama monastery of Yung-ho-kung. The lamassary was provided with sets of large ritual vessels in cloisonné. Bushell tells us[6] that there was a magnificent altar set of five vessels, consisting of an incense urn, two pricket candlesticks and two flower vases, over six feet high, set on carved marble pedestals in the principal courtyard of the monastery. He goes on to say, 'the Russians, who made the monastery their headquarters in 1900, are said to have carried off most of the cloisonné vessels, and this imposing row is now perhaps to be seen somewhere in St. Petersburg, if not at the Hermitage itself.' There are, in fact, some large vessels of this kind in the Hermitage, and if they could be shown to be the vessels presented to the Yung-ho-kung monastery by the Emperor Yung-chêng, a great step forward would be made in the identification of cloisonné of this period.

Hardly any pieces of cloisonné are known with the mark of K'ang-hsi and none with that of Yung-chêng. Thus the flower vase fitted with a liner, in the Freer Gallery of Art, Washington (Pl. 66) is of particular importance. It is in the form of an ancient bronze *ku* decorated with archaistic motives interspersed with floral scrolls. The floral motives are repeated on the liner, with seven apertures representing the flowers. The decoration shows little Ming influence and the scroll designs are similar to those found on many eighteenth-century pieces of cloisonné. The shape has an elegance that proclaims its Ch'ing origin. The piece has a mark, cast inside the base rim, which reads *Ta Ch'ing K'ang-hsi nien Wang Tzŭ-fan chih*, 'made by Wang Tzu-fan in the K'ang-hsi

[4] Soulié de Morant, *L'histoire de l'art chinois*, 1928.
[5] S. W. Bushell, *Chinese art*, 1910, Vol. II, p. 76.   [6] Reference 5.

THE CH'ING DYNASTY

period' (Pl. 96A). The colours of the enamels are dark blue, green, red, brown and white with a pale turquoise-blue ground. There is no trace of the rose-pink enamel derived from gold. Both the base of the piece and the wires are made of copper.[7]

If we accept this flower vase as a genuine production of the K'ang-hsi period — and there is every reason why we should do so — it tells us much about the introduction of new techniques in cloisonné manufacture in the Ch'ing dynasty. The absence of the rose-pink enamel is not surprising, because the development of this enamel had hardly reached the stage at which it would be available for use in cloisonné before the end of the reign of K'ang-hsi. The use of copper wire establishes that the change to copper from bronze had taken place long before the reign of Ch'ien-lung, when we know that the use of copper had become standardized. There is not sufficient evidence at present to tell us in which part of the K'ang-hsi reign the flower vase was made, but the resemblance of the scroll-work to that of marked Ch'ien-lung pieces favours a rather late date and suggests that the flower vase was made after rather than before 1700.

Thus although the vase throws valuable light on the date of the introduction of copper wires, we still need more evidence from other marked pieces, or from pieces otherwise datable. As has been said, it seems likely that the introduction of new techniques took place at the re-organization of the cloisonné industry when the imperial factory was set up round about 1680, and this is the most likely time for the introduction of copper wire, so much more easily and evenly produced by mass production wire-drawing methods. There is some evidence to support this from pieces with signs of Ming influence in the enamels which have copper wires. This matter is of great importance, because we have here one of the few revolutionary changes in methods of fabrication which can help more than any other factor in the dating of early Ch'ing cloisonné.

As we have said, no pieces of cloisonné are known with the reign marks of Yung-chêng (1723–35), but there can be no doubt that many pieces belonging to this reign are in existence, both in China and the West. We can be certain that the wires of these pieces are of copper and that many of them will have rose-pink enamels. The identification of these pieces, which are almost certainly attributed to the Ch'ien-lung period, cannot be achieved at present. But it should be possible to throw some further light on them by studying the pieces from the Yung-ho-kung and other famous temples known to have been favoured by the emperors K'ang-hsi and Yung-chêng. There should be documentary evidence of some of the presentations, but no information of this kind seems hitherto to have been published.

The two imposing Buddhist lion-dogs in the University Museum, Philadelphia, one of which is illustrated in Plate 73, must surely have

[7] The base and wires have both been analysed by the Brookhaven National Laboratory and found to contain over 99 per cent of copper.

THE CH'ING DYNASTY

been made for imperial presentation to a famous temple. They stand nearly eight feet in height and are the largest pieces of Chinese cloisonné recorded. Although each piece is made in five parts, the head of each lion-dog and its decorative collar being separate from the body and the stand being in two parts, the individual pieces are still of great size and would have required very large muffle furnaces for firing the enamels. The facilities needed and the cost of manufacture would have been far beyond what was possible in China except under the direct patronage of the emperor.

It was the practice in China from T'ang times onwards to use pairs of lions at the entrances of tombs and temples to guard them against evil spirits. The lion was not indigenous to China, and although lions were brought to China as presents to the emperor in Han times, the Chinese craftsmen were never very familiar with them and the models they made were unrealistic. They show some association, in T'ang times, with the Indian Buddhist lions but they gradually came to resemble closely the Pekingese pug, the so-called 'lion-dog'. In the Ch'ing dynasty they often appear in pairs, the male with his foot on a brocade ball and the female with a pup. The Philadelphia lion-dogs are such a pair.

The wires used in these figures are of bronze with a rather high silver content and the enamels, in Ming tradition, include a composite red and white (the so-called 'Ming pink') and a dark brown. The rose-pink enamel derived from gold is, as might be expected, missing. The technical features favour a late seventeenth- rather than an eighteenth-century date. No information seems to be available on the early history of these important pieces.

When we come to the Ch'ien-lung period we have a wealth of material, including many pieces with the mark either cast in the base and therefore contemporary, or incised and needing careful scrutiny. In a few rare examples the mark is set in enamel. A study of the marked pieces enables us to identify the particular characteristics of Ch'ien-lung cloisonné. The scroll designs are very consistent, the even double-lined stems being built up of elements of short length containing enamels of different colours, giving a gay but discontinuous effect. These elements are rarely joined together by solder. The enamel colours are quite distinctive. There is a dark turquoise-green, different from the dark green of the Ming dynasty, and a number of pale yellowish-green enamels. There are also some new purple and lilac shades. The cobalt-blue is a good colour, much better than we find in most of the later Ming wares. The rose-pink enamel is often present, but in some pieces it is omitted, as indeed it often is in the enamelled porcelain of the period. The wires, as has been pointed out already — but it is necessary to stress this, as a sure method of identification — are almost invariably of copper. The only exceptions in late cloisonné to this rule lie in a group of easily identified Ming imitations and a few pieces in which the wires are of gold. The depth of gold plating on the Ch'ien-

THE CH'ING DYNASTY

lung wires is often considerable and their basic material is not always evident.

A good deal has been said about the excellence of manufacture of the Ch'ien-lung cloisonné, and there is no doubt that the pieces of this period are, as a rule, very well made. But the alleged superiority, even in a technical sense, over the Ming wares, is based on a superficial study of the material and is largely due to the fact that the Ch'ien-lung cloisonné is generally in far better condition than the early wares. Most of the later wares have their enamels pitted in the same way as the earlier ones, but much care was given, at the time of manufacture, to filling in the holes with coloured wax and this has often survived far better than the fillings of the earlier wares.

Let us now look at some actual pieces of the Ch'ien-lung period. Two of the finest examples are a small vase (*hu*) in archaic bronze form and with archaistic decoration (Col. Pl. G) and a tankard with globular body and gilt-bronze handle in the form of a dragon, decorated with lotus scrolls round the body and formal borders above (Pl. 67A). This tankard is clearly derived from the early fifteenth-century blue and white tankards, such as the one illustrated by Brankston.[8] Both these pieces have a good deal of rose-pink enamel and the other enamels are entirely typical of the period. They both have the incised four-character mark *Ch'ien-lung nien chih*. Another unusually fine piece, not at all typical of the period, is the four-sided casket and cover, with finely cast gilt-bronze lion-handles and finial, which is decorated in Ming style in enamels resembling those of the fifteenth century (Pl. 67B). There are many points of detail which would rule out a Ming date for this piece, quite apart from its honest six-character Ch'ien-lung mark cast in the base (Pl. 96B). A close examination of the enamels reveals a few minute touches of the rose-pink enamel, showing the difficulty the eighteenth-century craftsman had in getting away from his familiar surroundings. This piece is also exceptional in not having the wires made of copper. A soft yellowish metal has been used which has not been analysed, but which may be gold. These three pieces, as fine in quality as anything produced in the Ch'ien-lung period, were bequeathed to the Victoria and Albert Museum by George Salting, whose excellent taste, in subjects outside Chinese porcelain, is not generally known to students of oriental art.

Another piece, with the four-character mark, is an incense burner in the form of a ram (Pl. 68B). The scroll designs and the enamels, with a good deal of the rose-pink, are typical of the period.

An extensive group of pieces, invariably decorated with formal lotus scrolls, consists of small vases, incense burners and boxes, sometimes grouped to form a set. Two typical pieces are shown in Plate 69A. A few pieces bear the contemporary cast mark integral with the piece but most of them bear the incised mark in four or six characters set in

---

[8] A. D. Brankston, *Early Ming wares of Chingtechen*, 1938, Pl. 4.

THE CH'ING DYNASTY

a horizontal line, with an additional character underneath.[9] Sometimes the additional character is simply a number, evidently identifying the piece as part of a set. At other times the character is clearly intended as a mark of commendation. In this class we find *yü*, 'jade', a character often found on blue and white porcelain of fine quality, and *lien*, 'pure' (Pl. 96D). In other marks again the significance of the character is obscure. The use of characters in addition to a *nien hao* seems to be peculiar to cloisonné. The marks, being incised, are not necessarily contemporary, but many of them are in excellent calligraphy and have good claims to be accepted. Others are perhaps doubtful, even though there can be no doubt that the pieces themselves are of the Ch'ien-lung period, or possibly, in some instances, even earlier.

A brief history of the development of the *ju-i* sceptre from early times was given in Chapter 8. In the eighteenth and nineteenth centuries the practice of giving these sceptres as birthday presents must, if we may judge from the large number of sceptres that have survived in jade, lacquer, porcelain and cloisonné enamel, have been very popular. A typical eighteenth-century cloisonné enamel sceptre is shown in Plate 69B. The enamel panel in the head is of gilt-copper, with bats in relief among scrolling clouds. The protuberances along the stem are typical of the later sceptres, in contrast with the more simple stems of the seventeenth century (Pls. 61A, B and C).

Many large and important vessels were made in this period, but they are rarely marked. Reference has already been made to the sets of large vessels made for ritual use in the reigns of K'ang-hsi and Yung-ch'êng for presentation by the emperor to Buddhist temples. The practice was continued in the reign of Ch'ien-lung and many sets date from this reign. That illustrated in Plate 70 is probably one of these. The large rectangular vessel with a perforated cover, supported by two kneeling figures (Pl. 71), was formerly used in the Imperial Summer Palace, near Peking, to hold blocks of ice to keep the air cool in the hot season. The large brazier, one of a pair (Pl. 72), is another fine example of the more ornate pieces made for the court.

Mention has been made of the figures of animals and birds that began to be made in the late sixteenth and early seventeenth centuries. These figures were made in great numbers in the eighteenth century, when models of quails, cranes and ducks were particularly in favour. Among the animals we find elephants, rams and buffaloes. Sometimes the figures are highly stylized, such as the incense burner in the form of a ram already described (Pl. 68B). At other times the treatment is naturalistic, as in the buffalo (Pl. 74A), in which the colours are simply white and aubergine with slight touches of red. The fine large pair of cranes (Pl. 75) and the pricket candlestick, in which the pricket is supported on the head of a duck with outstretched wings standing on a tortoise with a serpent intertwined (Pl. 74B) have good claims to be-

---

[9] Some of the marks are incised on rectangular gilt panels set in the enamel, and these have good claims to be contemporary.

G. CH'IEN-LUNG MARK AND PERIOD.   HEIGHT 5·1 in.
Victoria and Albert Museum
See p. 91

THE CH'ING DYNASTY

long to the Ch'ien-lung period. There are many later figures, belonging to the nineteenth century. Human figures are not common in cloisonné. The earliest examples seem to date from the seventeenth century, and the charming little boy with his hobby horse and dog (Pl. 76) is one of these. It was attributed to the late Ming dynasty in the O.C.S. Exhibition of 1957, but an early Ch'ing attribution now seems more likely. Religious figures were seldom made in cloisonné at any period, a surprising fact when one bears in mind the traditional use of cloisonné for religious ceremonial objects. For some reason, gilt-bronze figures were preferred.

Reference was made in the last chapter to the large brilliant panels made in the seventeenth century, mainly for insertion into pieces of furniture. Many large panels were made during the Ch'ing dynasty, and particularly in the Ch'ien-lung period, but these seem to have been made usually as complete pictures, for permanent display on walls in the Western manner. Some of them are known, as are similar panels in carved red lacquer and painted enamels, with contemporary frames. The panel in Plate 77, depicting a river landscape with the 'hundred deer', is a fine example of this type of panel. It bears on the back an inscription of a poem by the Emperor Ch'ien-lung, referring to the deer in the royal park with their young, free from fear, preserved by royal decree from the attack of the archers with their arrows.

The use of champlevé in Chinese enamelwork is not often found except as details in a cloisonné piece. The vessel in the form of a standing animal, possibly a ram, intended for use as a flower holder (Pl. 68A), is in champlevé, with some details in cloisonné. The colours are limited to green and red, with a little blue, and there is a mark set in enamel which reads *Ch'ien-lung fang ku*, 'Ch'ien-lung imitation of the antique', possibly an allusion to the fact that the piece is decorated broadly in late Chou style. This mark also occurs on porcelain bowls decorated in *famille rose* enamels with the dancing boy Chia Ch'ang with his hens and chickens.[10]

The technique known as repoussé was used very little before the eighteenth century, although a few Ming pieces are known in which the process is used for some details, particularly in perforated covers to vessels. In the Ch'ien-lung period repoussé came into general use, either by itself or in combination with cloisonné. In repoussé the enamels are not ground down to a smooth level surface, but left as they come from the fire with a pleasantly undulating surface. A fine example is the globular vase with raised trellis work and flowers (Pl. 79), which is in repoussé with some cloisonné details. Two colours shading effectively into each other are used in each flower. Another fine piece is the ten-lobed box decorated with flower sprays (Pl. 78), in which a single colour of enamel, a dark cobalt-blue, is used. This is entirely in repoussé. These two pieces are made with a base of copper sheet, gilded in the exposed places. Silver was also used for repoussé work, par-

[10] Reference 1, p. 34.

THE CH'ING DYNASTY

ticularly in the nineteenth century. But the silver bowl, decorated with engraved bats and clouds on a pale turquoise-blue enamel ground (Pl. 80A), has good claims to belong to the eighteenth century.

Cloisonné was used in China to a limited extent in conjunction with painted enamels, the usual arrangement being for the panels of figures, landscapes or flowers in painted enamels to be surrounded by scrolls in cloisonné. Sometimes the surrounding scrolls are merely in imitation of cloisonné with gold lines, representing the wires, painted on and fired. The double gourd vase (Pl. 81B) has true cloisonné surrounding the painted enamel panels. It bears the four-character Ch'ien-lung mark and certainly belongs to the period. A few rare examples are known in which the whole of the metalwork, including the wires, is of gold. One of these is a libation vessel (*chüeh*) with its stand (Pl. 81A), which has three depressions round the central boss into which the feet of the *chüeh* fit. This arrangement of *chüeh* and stand goes back at least to early Ming times. A fifteenth-century stand in blue and white porcelain, belonging to Mr. and Mrs. Frederick Mayer, has two five-clawed dragons swimming in swirling waves that break on the rock forming the central boss.[11] The gold and enamel *chüeh* and stand have a number of panels delicately painted with figures, landscapes and flowers in European style, surrounded by scrolls in cloisonné resembling closely those we find on Ch'ien-lung cloisonné on copper (see, for example, Pls. 68B, 69A). The base is marked with the four-character mark in enamel, and the *chüeh* has a similar incised mark. A somewhat similar *chüeh* and stand, in the Chinese Imperial Collection at Taiwan, is made, apparently, with a copper base.[12]

In Chapter 2 a short account was given of enamel techniques developed in Europe, in one of which a design is either carved out (*basse taille*) or built up by silver or gold foil underneath a translucent enamel. Pieces in the latter technique were made by the Chinese in the late eighteenth or early nineteenth centuries, and as they are more closely allied to cloisonné than to the painted enamels they call for a short account here. A typical example is the large dish (Pl. 82A), in which a background design of silver foil covered with a deep-blue enamel has superposed on it flower scrolls with enamels in green, aubergine and red, also applied over silver foil.[13] A portion of the undersurface, decorated with flower scrolls in silver foil, etched to show details of flowers and leaves, is shown in Plate 82B. This is a rather more elaborate treatment than we usually find in European work. A number of smaller dishes and bowls in this technique were also produced in China. Similar translucent enamels to those on the dish, applied to a silver base, were also used in China for the decoration of jewellery, small boxes and trinkets. A typical group of small pieces of

[11] *O.C.S. Catalogue of Chinese blue and white porcelain, 1953–1954*, No. 39, Pl. 8.
[12] *Chinese art treasures*, 1961–2, No. 215.
[13] The dish bears the mark in gold on the base *Kuang-tung t'ien yüan*, 'Kuang-tung celestial spring', possibly a place-name.

THE CH'ING DYNASTY

jewellery is shown in Plate 80B. Most of this work belongs to the early nineteenth century.

The end of the Ch'ien-lung period is supposed, by some writers on the subject, to have brought to an end the production of cloisonné of high quality. In the absence of any pieces with later marks than that of Ch'ien-lung we must base our views on stylistic grounds and a study of the enamelled porcelain of the nineteenth century, of which there are many marked examples. These do not suggest that there was any great deterioration in the quality of the enamels in the earlier part of the nineteenth century, although there was in the material of the porcelain itself. The enamels on the imperial porcelain, particularly in the so-called 'Peking bowls', are as good as they are in all but the best of the Ch'ien-lung porcelain and far better than the poor work that formed the greater part of the export wares of the eighteenth century. It is reasonable to suppose that the same qualities persisted, not only in the painted enamels on copper, but also in the cloisonné, for there can be no doubt that all these varieties of enamel were made in the same workshops in Peking.

It seems likely that the type of cloisonné produced in the nineteenth century was similar to the vase of Plate 83A. This vase, with lobed globular body decorated with lotus scrolls on a yellow ground, from the similarity of the enamels to those on Chia-ch'ing and Tao-kuang porcelain, may well be an early ninteenth-century piece, although the possibility of a slightly earlier date cannot be entirely excluded. It bears the incised mark 'Made by Li Lao-t'ien'. The *ju-i* sceptre (Pl. 83B) may also be attributed to the early nineteenth century.

Finally, reference must be made to a group of coarsely made bowls imitating Ming cloisonné of the sixteenth century, such as the bowl of Plate 31B. A typical example of one of these copies is the bowl in Plate 84A. In some respects these copies resemble the dishes of poor quality made in the late sixteenth century, which were mentioned in Chapter 7. In both, bronze wires and rims were used and the enamels are thin, so that the base metal shows through, especially if the piece has been subjected to hard use. But the copies can be easily distinguished from the originals, not only by the inferiority of the designs and the much more perfunctory scroll and brocade grounds but also by the fact that no solder is used to attach the wires to the base. The thin wires are more uniform in thickness than we find in Ming work and are clearly made by a wire-drawing process. Some of the copies have a bronze plate, inserted in the enamel on the base, bearing an incised inscription *fang Ming*, 'copy of Ming', often under a mandarin's hat (Pl. 84B). These copies probably belong to the end of the nineteenth century, and most of them appear to be of Chinese origin, although the possibility of Japanese copies cannot be entirely ruled out.

10. Japanese Cloisonné Enamels

The earliest piece of Japanese enamelwork known to us is a small hexagonal plaque, which is attributed to the Asuka period (A.D. 552–710). It was excavated from the Kengyūshi tomb, Sakaimura, Takaishi-son, in Nara prefecture (Pls. 85A, B). The decoration is provided by a six-petalled flower outlined by bronze walls that were originally gold plated. The cells inside these walls are filled with a red-brown translucent enamel and the flower is surrounded by an opaque sand-coloured enamel bearing a whitish film over most of the surface. The hexagonal edge is slightly raised, forming a wall to retain this enamel. The plaque has suffered a good deal through burial and it is not possible to say whether the corroded bronze borders of the central flower are in cloisonné or champlevé, or if in cloisonné how the wires were attached. Miss Dorothy Blair, who has studied the piece thoroughly,[1] is of the opinion that the enamel is formed of molten glass dropped from a glass rod heated in a flame. The view is supported by the presence of irregular spots where the glass rod may have broken away and by the fact that the enamel does not completely fill the interstices.

There is evidence, in the form of glass beads and lumps of unworked glass, that the manufacture of glass, in a very elementary form, was established in Japan by the seventh century. The glass was used for the decoration of swords and other objects, but there is no evidence of its use for glass vessels. The first literary reference to the manufacture of glass occurs in the Taihō Ritsuryō (the so-called 'Taihō code'), promulgated in the year A.D. 702.[2] Glass of this kind would have been suitable for the decoration of objects such as the plaque, and there is no reason to doubt the archaeological evidence that the plaque was made round about this period. There are a few examples of even more simple, and possibly earlier, work from Korea, in the form of jewellery, in which glass layers, insecurely attached, have been found in simple cells on a gold base.[3] It is possible that the method of manufacture was similar to that already described for the Japanese plaque and that the method was introduced into Japan from Korea.

The famous cloisonné enamel mirror in the Shōsō-in has already been

[1] Dorothy Blair, 'The cloisonné-backed mirror in the Shōsō-in', *Journal of Glass Studies*, Vol. II, 1960.

[2] Reference 1. According to George Sampson, *Japan: a short cultural history*, 1931 (p. 156), the exact terms of the Taihō code are unknown, since it is preserved only in a commentary of A.D. 833, the *Rizo no Gige*.   [3] Reference 1.

briefly referred to.[4] In the past it has been discussed a good deal by Western experts on enamels, largely because of the possibility of its being of Chinese manufacture and belonging to the T'ang dynasty. While there are, as we shall see, considerable differences of opinion on the date of manufacture of the mirror, the view that it is T'ang is not, as far as I am aware, supported today by any authority on Chinese art of this period.

The Shōsō-in, part of the great Tōdaiji Monastery at Nara, is a simple wooden storehouse, built in the eighth century to contain the imperial treasures belonging to the Emperor Shōmu, who died in A.D. 756. A few years previously, in 749, the colossal gilt-bronze statue of Vairocana Buddha, over fifty feet high, had been made and installed in a special building, the Hall of the Daibutsu. On the Emperor's death his widow, the Empress Kōmyō, dedicated to the great Buddha the national treasures formerly belonging to the Emperor. Many of these pieces are described in early inventories and have an unbroken history from the eighth century up to the present day. These relics are of outstanding importance in providing a vivid picture of the life of imperial Japan in the eighth century. But in the Shōsō-in there are many pieces recorded as having been deposited at a later date and there are others again which appear only to be recorded in late inventories, with no record of their deposition.

The judgments of early Western writers on the mirror were strongly influenced by the view then held that the presence of the mirror in the Shōsō-in provided certain evidence that it was placed there in the eighth century. Hobson, for example, accepted 'the unimpeachable Japanese authority that none of the Shōsō-in treasures are later than the eighth century'.[5] Gallois also accepted this view[6] and with some reluctance suggested a T'ang attribution for the mirror. But the thorough studies of Sir Percival David[7] have made it clear that a number of objects were deposited on dates from 818 to 1413. The latest deposition was of an octagonal mirror which was found under the floor of the Sugimoto Shrine and deposited during the present century, in 1902. It was shown for a time in the South Section of the Shōsō-in with other mirrors. Sir Percival David concludes, 'It is false to argue, as has been done more than once, that because an object is in the Shōsō-in, it is demonstrably anterior to the ninth century.' As for the cloisonné mirror itself, there is no record of its deposition. It might be argued from this that it is one of the eighteen mirrors recorded in the inventory, dated 1117, of objects in the South Section of the Shōsō-in. But the apparent absence of any subsequent records of the mirror does not inspire much confidence in this view. The South Sec-

[4] Chapter 3.
[5] R. L. Hobson, 'On Chinese cloisonné enamel', *Burlington Magazine*, 1912.
[6] H. C. Gallois, 'About T'ang and Ta Ts'in', *O.C.S.Transactions*, 1935.
[7] For a full account of the construction, dedication and subsequent history of the Shōsō-in, see Sir Percival David's 'The Shōsō-in', *Transactions and Proceedings of the Japan Society*, Vol. XXVIII, 1931.

tion, unlike the rest of the Shōsō-in, which was under an imperial seal, was under ecclesiastical control until 1836 and it would have been easier to add pieces to this Section than to the rest. Chait's view[8] that any evidence from the Shōsō-in should be discarded in assessing the date of the mirror has not, as far as is known, been met by any attempt to provide evidence of its early manufacture. It would seem therefore that it would be rash to base any views on the date of the mirror on the evidence at present available from the Shōsō-in itself. We must rely on the study of the piece itself and a comparison with pieces whose dates of manufacture are more precisely known.

The most complete description of the mirror is that given by Miss Dorothy Blair.[9] It is made basically of silver, the back of the mirror being decorated with enamels. The decoration is of a twelve-pointed lotus flower outlined in silver-gilt wires and filled in with translucent enamels in two shades of green and an opaque brown enamel (Pl. 5A). The small triangular pieces between the tips of the petals are of gold decorated with impressed nipples. The mirror has been built up of thirty-one separate parts, which have been cemented to the silver base with some form of lacquer. These thirty-one pieces are the central boss, the six surrounding leaflets, the six larger leaflets outside these with six others between, represented as seen partially behind them, and the twelve triangular gold pieces. The bases of the leaflets are of silver and the edges are turned up to provide pans to contain the enamels. The rest of the decoration is provided by wires, which, as far as can be judged from photographs of the mirror, are not attached by solder. The method of attachment of the wires is one feature not commented on by Miss Blair in her otherwise exhaustive and admirable description. It is of considerable importance as a factor in the assessment of the provenance of the mirror. The enamels, left as they emerged from the fire, unpolished, lie in translucent concave pools below the edges of the wires.

We can rule out right away any idea that the mirror could be of Western manufacture. The method of attachment of the components to the silver base by lacquer is sufficient by itself to establish an Eastern origin. Other features of the mirror that distinguish it from early Western enamels, such as those of Byzantium, are the use of translucent enamels, the wide spacing of the wires and the fact that the enamels are not polished to give a flat surface. Indeed, with the wide spacing adopted it is certain that any attempt to grind the enamels would have met with disaster. A comparison of the illustration of this mirror (Pl. 5A) with those of typical Byzantine pieces (Pls. 4A, B) shows how entirely different they are.

An early Chinese origin is, as we have said, no longer accepted by

[8] R. M. Chait, 'Some comments on the dating of early Chinese cloisonné, *Oriental Art*, Vol. III, No. 2, 1950.
[9] Reference 1. The best reproductions of the mirror (two in colour) are given in the *Shōsō-in Gyobutsu Zuroku*, Vol. XIV.

JAPANESE CLOISONNÉ ENAMELS

any authority on early Chinese art. In spite of the superficial points of resemblance between the decoration of the mirror and that on T'ang glazed dishes with incised designs,[10] no T'ang mirror with a design remotely resembling that of the enamelled mirror is known. Indeed there is no example of a twelve-pointed mirror of any kind in this dynasty. As for the possibility of the mirror being of later Chinese manufacture,[11] all the Chinese cloisonné made before the eighteenth century follows closely the Western techniques with closely spaced wires and opaque or semi-opaque enamels carefully ground flat and polished after being fired.

The degree of sophistication and the evidence of mass production methods used in the manufacture of the mirror suggest, to the author, a late date of manufacture. The mirror is made of a number of elements repeated with such precision as to suggest that they were made in jigs or templates. The thickness of the wires is remarkably even and it seems likely that they were not hand-made from ingots in the traditional method described by Theophilus as practised by the Byzantines,[12] and followed by the Chinese up to the seventeenth century,[13] but made by drawing the material through a die. There are, in fact, none of the qualities of hand craftsmanship that we find so prominently displayed, for example, in Chinese cloisonné enamels of the fifteenth century. It has been suggested that the fact that the enamels do not fill the cells and are left unpolished is an indication of an early technique. But in fact this is the first stage of any enamelling process and examples are known, both in Chinese and Japanese cloisonné, in which the enamels are left in this state. They may generally be unfinished pieces but there are a few in which the process was adopted deliberately. Several later Japanese pieces are known in which both processes were used in the same piece.[14] A final point bearing on the date of manufacture is the absence of solder, suggesting that the wires were secured in place by vegetable adhesives before the enamels were fired. This technique, in Chinese cloisonné, does not occur before the second half of the seventeenth century.

All the internal evidence suggests, to the author, that the mirror is of Japanese manufacture, made not earlier than the end of the seventeenth century and probably later than this. But this opinion is based on close examination of photographs and data provided from written descriptions and not on a study of the piece itself. Mr. Basil Gray, who has examined the mirror, considers that it belongs to the Momoyama period (1568–1615) and was probably made in the early seventeenth century. There is a strong tradition in Japan that much cloisonné was made in the Momoyama period and a number of examples are attributed to it. We shall now consider these and later examples and come back finally to the mirror, to see how it fits into the general scheme.

There are two specially important pieces of cloisonné in Japan

[10] See Reference 6.   [11] See Reference 8.   [12] See p. 23.   [13] See Chapter 4.
[14] An example is illustrated in L. F. Day, *Enamelling*, 1907, Pl. 63.

JAPANESE CLOISONNÉ ENAMELS

which seem to have strong claims to belong to the Momoyama period. The first of these is a crucifix in the Osaka City Museum (Pl. 85c). The ground colour is white and the emblems of the crucifixion, in four foliate panels, are in colours. It would seem that this crucifix must have been made before 1614, when the anti-Christian edict was promulgated. The enamels appear to be opaque and to follow closely those used in China in the seventeenth century. The second piece is the door handle of the main hall (Honden) of the Tōshōgū Shrine at Nikko, which was constructed as the mausoleum of Shogun Ieyasu, who died in 1616. The handle is decorated with translucent enamels that include a ruby red.

The Japanese traditions are not very helpful in enabling us to trace the development of enamels from the earliest times. The term *shippō*, used in Japan to describe enamels, literally means 'seven precious things'. It was used originally to describe a group of materials including gold, silver, and various jewels whose identity is a little uncertain. As in most countries, precious stones were first used for the decoration of metalwork, to be replaced later by glass and enamels. There are a number of references in the Japanese literature to the early manufacture of enamels in Japan. Most of them are fanciful and unsupported either by contemporary evidence or by any material that exists today. The earliest Japanese work that gives us some solid evidence, although mixed with a good deal of legend, is the *Sōken Kishō*,[15] a book mainly devoted to sword furniture, published in 1781. The following extract illustrates the mixture of fact and fancy that faces the student of the subject:

'Hikoshirō, of the Hirata family, *shippō* maker in the service of the Tokugawa, lived in the sixth street of Yushima, Yedo.

'What is known as *shippō* was introduced from abroad and the name may not be the original [foreign] name, but may have been given by us [the Japanese].[16]

'The *shippō wan* of the emperor of Sui [the Chinese dynasty, A.D. 569–618] was probably of the seven treasures. So called *shippō* is of gold, silver, *ruri* [glass or a green gem], *hari* [crystal], *shako* [coral], *meno* [agate] and pearl, but whether *shippō* was always made of these, or whether it was merely the name by which it was called, I cannot say.

'However this may be, there are many engaged in this art at present, but none of them is equal to Hikoshirō, whose splendid works may be considered superior to those which were imported.'

From this work we may certainly deduce that the making of enamel was well established by 1781 and that the Hirata family was the most

[15] This is fully discussed in J. L. Bowes, *Notes on Shippō*, 1895.
[16] The translation of the passage from the *Sōken Kishō* is that given by Bowes. I am indebted to Mr. William Watson for the checking of the translation which, except for this rather obscure sentence, is accurate. The sentence actually implies that *shippō* was the name given by the Japanese, but that there are good grounds for thinking that this is the correct name.

JAPANESE CLOISONNÉ ENAMELS

skilled in the art. The family was founded by Dōnin (1595–1646) and it is known that the name of Hikoshirō was used by him. But this name was also assumed by most of his successors and it must be one of these who is meant by the author of the *Sōken Kishō*. Bowes, who seems to have studied the history of the family very thoroughly,[17] states that Narihisa, the grandson of Dōnin, was the first member of the family to live in the sixth street of Yushima and that Nariyuki, the great-grandson of Narihisa, who died in 1769, was the last.

A number of pieces of sword furniture bearing the signature of different members of the Hirata family, from Dōnin, the founder of the family, to Nariyuki (the second member of this name), who died in 1890, are known. They are perhaps the most attractive of the Japanese enamels. The enamels themselves consist of miniature plaques or medallions, seldom more than half an inch across, in gold or silver-gilt cloisonné with translucent enamels. These plaques are made separately and then cemented or pressed into recesses in the sword fittings. The enamels are green, yellow, purple, white, red and blue, generally applied to a silver base and highly polished to give great brilliance. A careful study of examples in Western collections does not bring to light any distinguishing features between those bearing the earlier and later marks. Moreover the fact that enamels can be inserted into older sword guards — and a number of such insertions were undoubtedly made — adds to the difficulty of dating. The absence of any pieces in Western collections which can be attributed to a date earlier than the second half of the eighteenth century does not necessarily imply that none exist and it may be that authentic examples made by earlier members of the Hirata family exist in Japan or even, unrecognized, in Western collections.[18] The sword guard (*tsuba*) in Plate 86A is a typical example of the fine work of members of the Hirata family. It is by Hirata Narisuke, who died in 1816. It is inlaid with small panels of translucent cloisonné enamel and minute spirals of gold wire. Another sword guard in which the enamelwork was by the same worker bears an inscription stating that the guard was made by Yukimitsu, living at Hagi, Nagato province, while on the opposite side is an inscription 'made by Hirata Narisuke', clearly referring to the enamelwork. The two sides of the guard are shown respectively in Plates 87A and 87B. Although double signatures of this kind are extremely rare, it would seem that generally the enamelled decoration on this type of sword guard was done by a different workman from the one who actually made the guard. A number of pieces of sword furniture in this style, bearing the names of many members of the Hirata family, from the founder Dōnin down to Nariyuki II are known. But there are other pieces with the signatures of enamellers not belonging

[17] Reference 15.
[18] B. W. Robinson. *The arts of the Japanese sword*, 1961, illustrates a number of examples of enamelled sword furniture (Pl. 85). He considers that translucent enamels first appeared about 1770.

JAPANESE CLOISONNÉ ENAMELS

to this distinguished family[19] and many others not signed by the enameller at all. The circular sword guard of Colour Plate H, made of iron and finely decorated with cloisonné panels of larger size than usual, representing musical instruments, bears the signature of Tokinaga of Kōfu (a synonym of Yedo). Tokinaga was the maker of the guard itself, and it is likely that the enamels were inserted a little later, in the first half of the nineteenth century. Another sword guard, decorated with maple leaves and dewdrops, has some of the leaves in cloisonné enamel (Pl. 86B). The guard has the signature of Tozanshi (Nagahide) and probably belongs to the middle of the nineteenth century. Once again the enamelwork may be a little later than the guard itself.

There are a number of other pieces of enamelled sword furniture which have the appearance of being earlier than the delicate enamel work just described. One group is made of cast bronze,[20] decorated in champlevé with opaque enamels limited to dark green, pale yellow and a dull white. A typical example is decorated with lion-dogs and peonies (Pl. 88A). This group is traditionally supposed to be derived from Korean work and is known by the name 'Hirado', from the port on the west coast of Japan which dealt with trade from Korea. The Hirado group are somewhat primitive in appearance and there has been a tendency among collectors to attribute them to the seventeenth century. But they are not likely to have been made before the middle of the eighteenth century.

Two sword guards, also in champlevé and with opaque enamels limited to a very few colours, may perhaps be earlier than those in the group just described. The first is the iron guard of Plate 88C, decorated with magic cloaks in an overlay design in gold and silver, with the champlevé enamels confined to dark bluish-green. This could possibly be as early as the seventeenth century. The second is also of iron, decorated with a number of objects in raised bronze, with champlevé in dark yellowish-green, with small touches of white (Pl. 88B). The objects include a tobacco pouch, *inro* and accessories, all tied together by strings represented in red enamel. This is thought to be an early eighteenth-century piece.

With the evidence of all these pieces in front of us, the closest resemblance to the Shōsō-in mirror seems to be provided by the small cloisonné panels made by the members of the Hirata family as inlays for sword furniture. These panels are of course very much smaller than the mirror, but the use of translucent enamels, in which green plays a prominent part, on a silver background with silver gilt wires in these small panels is exactly the same technique as that adopted in the mirror. Is it possible that the mirror was made by some member of the distinguished Hirata family?

[19] Some of these are mentioned in H. L. Joly and K. Tomita, *Japanese art and handicraft*, 1916.
[20] The yellow alloy used for these pieces is known by the term *Sentoku*, the Japanese rendering of the characters for Hsüan-tê, so-called because it is supposed to have been invented in this reign.

H. EARLY NINETEENTH CENTURY. HEIGHT 3·0 in.
See p. 102

JAPANESE CLOISONNÉ ENAMELS

All the Japanese enamels that have been discussed so far were made as decorative objects and particularly for use in sword furniture, in contrast with the almost exclusive use of enamels in China for vessels, generally made for religious ceremonial purposes. The manufacture of Japanese cloisonné vessels seems to have occurred later than that of other pieces. The dating of these vessels has been the subject of so much controversy in the past that it is necessary here to go through the literature of the nineteenth century, when the controversy, at times very acrimonious, took place. J. L. Bowes, one of the pioneer collectors and students of Japanese enamels, put forward views which are almost completely discredited today.[21] He divided Japanese cloisonné vessels into three groups, 'early', 'middle period' and 'late'. He considered that the 'early' group go back to the sixteenth century and the 'middle period' group to the eighteenth. Let us look at the wares of the 'middle period' first. A typical example is shown in Plate 90. These wares were greatly admired by a number of Western collectors during the second half of the nineteenth century. To us today they have little to commend them. The shapes are often ungainly and the decoration crowded and meaningless, while the colours are dull when compared with those of Chinese cloisonné. The enthusiasm of Western collectors for these wares, as well as for other contemporary objects of Japanese art such as the meretricious Satsuma pottery, is difficult to understand. Bowes's admiration for the 'middle period' *shippō* led him to put forward a theory that the pieces were made in a special factory for the imperial court during the eighteenth century and were not released to the public until the breakdown of the feudal system in the mid-nineteenth century.

Brinkley, who also devoted some study to Japanese enamels, entirely disagreed with the views put forward by Bowes. Brinkley's view[22] was that the use of early enamels in Japan was confined to accessories such as sword furniture, beads, clasps and the recessed handles of sliding doors. He suggests that the introduction of enamels into Japan may have come from Korea and he mentions that cloisonné enamelling was well understood by the Koreans in the sixteenth century, if not earlier, twisted wires being used to form the cells.[23] Brinkley's main point of disagreement with Bowes is on the date of manufacture of the cloisonné vessels. Brinkley suggests that it was not until 1839 that such vessels were made in Japan. If this is true, the reasons why the Japanese who were, as the references in Japanese literature show, familiar with Chinese cloisonné of the Ming dynasty, should not have attempted to make similar pieces requires some explanation. Brinkley provides this by saying that such vessels were not suitable for the tea ceremony, which dominated the Japanese attitude towards works of art.

[21] Reference 15.   [22] F. Brinkley, *Japan and China*, Vol. 7, 1904.
[23] There seems to be no factual evidence to support Brinkley's views on Korean cloisonné.

JAPANESE CLOISONNÉ ENAMELS

According to Brinkley, the first Japanese to make cloisonné vessels was Kaji Tsunekichi, who succeeded in 1839 in making plates and other objects which were presented to the Tokugawa court in Yedo by the feudal chief of Owari as examples of the technical achievements of Kaji. In 1853 Kaji began to take pupils and by 1858, when foreign merchants began to settle in Yokohama, cloisonné vessels in some quantity began to be made for the foreign market. It may be noted that the most important collection of Japanese cloisonné built up in the nineteenth century, that of J. L. Bowes, was acquired mainly between the years 1867 and 1874. According to Bowes, the supply of what he calls 'ancient and genuine pieces', in which he included the 'middle period' wares, had almost ceased by 1874.

With this historical background let us look at a few examples of the 'middle period' wares. The dish of Plate 90 is typical of the best of these. Three small circular panels of pine, bamboo and plum are surrounded by groups of repetitive florets, diapers and leaf scrolls arranged in a haphazard manner. The box in Plate 91B shows an even more eccentric arrangement. The colours of the enamels are varied, but the absence of a good turquoise-blue, the most important feature of Chinese cloisonné enamels, makes the Japanese work look rather sombre. In spite of this the pieces have a gaudy effectiveness which was no doubt responsible for their appeal to the Western collectors of the nineteenth century. But the designs surely represent the low water of oriental decorative art. Even worse than the decoration are the shapes of some of the vases, which are as ugly as anything ever produced in Japan, or indeed anywhere (Pl. 91A).

There can be no doubt, in spite of Bowes's enthusiastic claims, that the 'middle period' wares belong to the mid-nineteenth century. They probably include the pieces first made by Kaji Tsunekichi, as mentioned by Brinkley, in 1839, and it would seem that the manufacture had virtually ceased by 1874. A study of the workmanship shows that these wares are the product of a machine age. The repetitive patterns are clearly adapted for mass production and superficially the workmanship is of a high standard. But the bases of dishes, bowls and vases and the interiors of boxes are covered with a single application of badly fitting dark green enamel, uneven in surface and generally unsupported by wires. In the cloisonné decoration, as in all Japanese work, the wires are held in place by the enamels alone, except for the slight use of solder, in a few exceptional pieces, to secure one wire to another. The use of a temporary adhesive in the early stages of manufacture is indicated.

Let us now look at Bowes's 'early period' wares. They form a small group resembling closely some of the sixteenth-century Chinese cloisonné pieces, typified by the two large dishes of Plates 48 and 49. Bowes himself mixed up the two groups and in his illustration of five early pieces in his collection,[24] one piece is certainly a late sixteenth-

[24] J. L. Bowes, *Japanese enamels*, 1886, Pl. IV.

JAPANESE CLOISONNÉ ENAMELS

century Chinese dish and one of the four bowls is probably Chinese, while the three remaining bowls are Japanese. These pieces were sold in Liverpool with the rest of the collection in 1901 and few of them can be located today. But one of these bowls was purchased by the Victoria and Albert Museum and as a typical piece of the 'early period' is of some importance (Pl. 89B). It is decorated with four seated sages against a background of clouds, in colours more sober than those of the Chinese wares. In particular one misses the bright turquoise-blue that forms the background of most of the Chinese pieces. The thin bronze wires are held in place only by the enamels, no solder being used. While the workmanship compares unfavourably in some respects with that of the Chinese originals, it is far superior to the meretricious cloisonné of the 'middle period'. The bowl is a piece of honest craftsmanship in which the metalworker has laid out his design with some sense of purpose. It may be noted that the base of this piece is finished in the same style as the rest of the piece and not perfunctorily as in the 'middle period' wares. The small vase, decorated with lotus scrolls on a white ground (Pl. 89A), belongs to the same group.

There is a temptation to follow Bowes in dating the 'early period' wares as contemporary with the Chinese originals. But it is doubtful whether the Japanese cloisonné are earlier than the eighteenth century. It was at this time that Japanese interest in late Ming porcelain was great, and many copies of the Wan-li five-coloured wares were made. It is possible that the cloisonné wares under discussion arise from the same interest in the Wan-li period.

Towards the end of the nineteenth century an entirely new school of enamelworkers was set up in Japan, the leading worker being Namikawa Yasuyuki of Kyoto. The new cloisonné reached a higher standard than in any previous Japanese work, except possibly the best work of the Hirata school. The colours of the enamels are in great variety and the fine wire-work is applied with great precision. These pieces are generally decorated with subjects such as growing plants or landscapes with flowers, birds and butterflies, treated in a naturalistic style. The treatment is much closer to that of painted enamels than had been attempted in earlier Chinese and Japanese cloisonné. The wires are unobtrusive, being often silvered rather than gilt, and left in a dull black unpolished state. The elegant vase, decorated with wistaria in mauve and green shades against a pale grey ground (Pl. 92), is an example of this type at its best. The bowl with bamboo leaves in shades of mauve (Pl. 93B) has a contrasting translucent crimson enamel inside, covering a leaf design on a mottled ground, apparently produced by a repoussé process.

Sometimes the Japanese enamellers went a step further towards the painted enamels by using wires to locate the enamel pastes and removing them before the piece was fired. This process was sometimes repeated several times in the manufacture of a piece. This type of enamel is known in Japan as *musen-shippō*, 'cloisonless enamels'.

JAPANESE CLOISONNÉ ENAMELS

The leading exponent of this class of work was Namikawa Sosuke of Tōkyō. Another type of enamel, requiring great technical skill, is that known in the West as *plique à jour*, and in Japan as *shotai-shippō*, in which the enamels have no base and the light can shine through as it does in stained glass. A typical example is shown in Plate 93A.

Finally, reference should be made to the use of cloisonné techniques on porcelain. The wires are cemented in place on the already fired porcelain base, filled in with the glass pastes and fired in the usual way. The earliest use of the method, if we may judge by the style of brocade decoration adopted, is round about the middle of the nineteenth century.[25] But the more usual types are decorated in naturalistic style, like the latest cloisonné, the wires being finished in dull silver. The box in Plates 94A, B, has a mark which indicates that it was made by Ishijio of Hara, Aichi-Ken (the Owari province of feudal times). It probably belongs to the late nineteenth century.

[25] S. W. Bushell, *Oriental ceramic art*, 1899, p. 730, credits the workshops of Nagoya with the invention soon after 1870.

Appendix 1

MARKS ON CLOISONNÉ ENAMELS

THE marks on cloisonné enamels can either be cast, incised or incorporated in the enamel itself. Incised marks can have been made at any time but cast marks and marks in enamel, at first sight, would seem to be above suspicion. But it is a comparatively easy matter to add additional bases with marks on them to pieces of cloisonné. Moreover, if these bases are fitted skilfully it is difficult to detect that they are not original. Many pieces with added bases on which cast or incised marks have been applied are known, and in some of them the additions have been so cunningly made that very close study has been necessary to expose them. Pieces with added enamel marks have not been recorded, but it is always desirable to make certain, in such marks, that they are not on separate pieces of metal which could have been added.

Thus, if one is to place any confidence in a mark on cloisonné, it is necessary first of all to be quite certain that the mark is contemporary. If it is, can we deduce anything from the calligraphy? In porcelain, a good deal of weight has been rightly attached by connoisseurs to the calligraphy of marks. But there is a great difference between the freedom in calligraphy obtained by the brush work of a painter and the best that can be achieved by a skilled worker in metal.

In porcelain, there is plenty of evidence to support the view that the marks were painted by specially selected craftsmen. The making of a piece of porcelain was entrusted to a large number of workmen, each responsible for a small specialized job. Père d'Entrecolles tells us that in the early eighteenth century[1] as many as seventy craftsmen were engaged in making a single piece of porcelain, each of whom was responsible for a single process, such as the single line encircling the rim of a vessel. Among these craftsmen the calligraphers who added the marks must have occupied an important position. In the marks of the imperial wares of the Ming dynasty we can see evidence of the individual hand of the painter, with peculiarities in the repetition of particular characters. This is especially noticeable in the marks of the Chêng-tê period, where the calligraphy of the imperial wares decorated with five-clawed dragons is quite different from that of the so-called 'Mohammedan wares'.[2] But we must not lose sight of the fact that

[1] S. W. Bushell, *A description of Chinese pottery and porcelain, being a translation of the T'ao Shuo*, 1910, p. 190.
[2] See the author's *Oriental blue and white*, 1954, Ch. 12.

APPENDIX 1

many excellent copies of the earlier marks were made. The painter who could simulate the characteristics of fifteenth-century painting in blue and white porcelain is not likely to have found the calligraphy of the marks particularly difficult to copy. The marks should therefore only be regarded as providing a small part of the total evidence necessary to identify the piece.

In cloisonné, the evidence of the calligraphy is far less positive than it is in porcelain. Incised marks, in which the individuality of the craftsman is allowed some scope, provide the nearest approach to painted marks on porcelain. Moulded marks, although obtained in the first place from an incised mark, are a stage removed from the individuality of the original maker of the mark. As for marks made in cloisonné or champlevé in the enamel, the laborious methods employed are so far removed from the spontaneity of the painter of calligraphy as to render them of little value as a means of assessment.

The calligraphy of the *nien hao* of Ching-t'ai requires special mention. In Chapter 6 we have shown that the mark of this emperor was not used on cloisonné before the seventeenth century. Yet the Ching-t'ai marks on many pieces were accepted by Chinese experts in the past, as is shown by the number of such pieces handed down in the Chinese Imperial Collection. Three examples of the marks of this reign are shown in Plates 95D, 95G and 95H. The first, incised on the base of the vase of Plate 20, has always been regarded as a very good example of incised calligraphy. The second and third are moulded marks. The former, a six-character mark, is on the base of the *kuei* of Plate 21A, and the latter, a four-character mark, is on the base of the *kuei* of Plate 21B. These three pieces are of particular interest because they all belong to the fifteenth century, but are fitted with bases added in the late seventeenth or early eighteenth century. A number of pieces in the Chinese Imperial Collection, none of which have any claims to belong to the fifteenth century, bear similar marks.

This evidence of the calligraphy of Ching-t'ai marks is disquieting, because it throws doubt on the reliability of experts who have accepted the calligraphy of pieces in the Chinese Imperial Collection. We are accustomed in the West to a healthy distrust of handwriting experts, whose conflicting evidence has been exposed on so many occasions. But we have been prepared to regard as sacrosanct the pronouncements of Chinese and Japanese experts on calligraphy. Perhaps our attitude should be more critical.

We can turn with more satisfaction to some of the marks of the Hsüan-tê period. Four of these are set in enamel and are therefore contemporary with the piece. In three of them, the ritual disc (Pl. 10A), box and cover (Pls. 11A, B) and large jar (Pls. 12, 13A, B, C) the marks are in champlevé, a process that does not lend itself to flowing calligraphy. All these pieces belong to the fifteenth century and reasons have been given in Chapter 5 for thinking that the first two pieces belong to the period of the mark, while the jar is a little later. The fourth

APPENDIX 1

piece, the dish or cup-stand of Colour Plate B, has an incised mark on the base which has been filled in with dark blue enamel (Pl. 95A). The calligraphy is seen to be close to that of a blue and white dish of the period (Pl. 95B).

Two other marks of the Hsüan-tê period are worthy of mention. The mark on the box of Plate 26B, illustrated in Plate 95c, is rather carelessly incised in a calligraphy with none of the qualities normally associated with the fifteenth century. It is almost certainly an addition of the seventeenth or eighteenth century. The double-lined mark on the dish or cup-stand of Plate 22, on the other hand, is in a different class. The mark (Pl. 95E) has been incised with great skill and it is possible that it belongs, if not to the period of the mark, to the fifteenth century. But equally skilful marks of the Wan-li period in double-lined characters (Pl. 95F) raise some doubt on the mark of the earlier reign.

We have mentioned the Chia-ching marks, all of which are incised, in Chapter 7. The example shown in Plate 38B is typical. The calligraphy is not unlike that to be found on porcelain and lacquer of the Chia-ching period. By itself, the mark would not, in view of what has already been said, be expected to carry much weight. But the pieces themselves are typical of sixteenth-century work. Moreover, the reign of Chia-ching has no reputation for cloisonné and there would seem to have been little inducement to add marks of this period later. These points are by no means conclusive, but on balance there is a strong bias in favour of the marks being contemporary.

The Wan-li marks, on the other hand, being in enamel, can be accepted without any reservation. Two of the marked pieces, illustrated in Colour Plate F and Plate 47A, are typical in every way. The marks are all in the form *Ta Ming Wan-li tsao* (Pls. 47B, c). The use of the character *tsao* in place of *chih* is not common in imperial wares, such as the dish of Colour Plate F undoubtedly is, but occasional examples of the mark in blue and white imperial porcelain are known.

When we come to the Ch'ing dynasty, we find large numbers of pieces with the Ch'ien-lung mark and hardly any belonging to the other reigns of the dynasty. The K'ang-hsi mark rarely occurs on cloisonné, so that the mark on the flower holder of Plate 66 is of special importance. It is cast on the inside of the base rim (Pl. 96A) and must be contemporary with the piece. The inscription reads *Ta Ch'ing K'ang-hsi nien Wang Tzu-fan chih*, (made by Wang Tzu-fan in the K'ang-hsi period). Several pieces are known with the incised mark of K'ang-hsi. One of these is a large incense burner supported on three elephants heads in gilt-bronze, illustrated and described by Hobson,[3] which bears the six-character mark on the rim. This piece is one of a pair, which no doubt once formed part of a Buddhist altar set. The piece may possibly belong to the K'ang-hsi period but we cannot use the incised mark as evidence. A number of other pieces are known with

[3] R. L. Hobson, 'On Chinese cloisonné enamel, *Burlington Magazine*, Vol. XXI, 1912.

APPENDIX 1

marks in enamel carrying a specific year-mark, but these appear to be much later than the period.

No pieces are known with the Yung-chêng mark, but there is a wealth of material belonging to the Ch'ien-lung period. Most of the marks of this reign are incised but there are a few moulded marks, such as the six-character mark illustrated in Plate 96B, belonging to the casket of Plate 67B and the four-character mark of Plate 96c. The incised marks are sometimes made on a rectangular panel set in the enamel, but more often are found on the base of the piece. The marks are sometimes in four characters placed in a double square (Pl. 96E) and sometimes in four or six characters set in a horizontal line. In addition we often find an additional character placed underneath. Sometimes it apparently indicates a mark of commendation such as *lien* (Pl. 96D), 'pure', *jên*, 'benevolence', and *yü*, 'jade'. The last character is often to be found in blue and white porcelain of fine quality. At other times the additional character simply indicates a number. Numbers up to five have been recorded, and it seems likely that they indicate that the piece is part of a set. Additional characters such as these seem to be peculiar to cloisonné and it is possible that some of them were added later.

Appendix 2

SPLIT WIRES IN CHINESE CLOISONNÉ ENAMELS

OBSERVATION has shown that in pieces of Ming cloisonné enamels a proportion of the wires have longitudinal cracks. The cracks are sometimes short in length but they often extend along the whole or greater part of the wire. In some pieces as many as half of the wires are found to be affected, but the proportion is generally much less than this. Every piece with claims to be Ming which it has been possible to examine carefully has been found to have some split wires. The cracks, however, are often completely covered over by gilding and are also not easy to detect when the wires are dirty. Nevertheless, it is remarkable that, so far as is known to the author, no previous writer has drawn attention to this very evident characteristic.

In some of the wires the cracks run almost uniformly along the middle of the wire, giving the impression that two wires are placed side by side, or that a single wire has been bent round, showing the two edges side by side. These effects are shown clearly in Plate 8, in which is shown a small part of a bowl magnified four times. The regularity of the cracks makes it difficult, at first sight, to reject the idea that they were caused by some manipulation of the material by the craftsman. Nevertheless, a study of a number of pieces led the author to the conclusion, before any experiments were attempted, that the cracks were the result of some defect in the material of the wire, and not the deliberate work of the craftsman. It was not clear, however, whether the cracks were present at the time of manufacture of the piece or whether they were caused by subsequent corrosive action. The metallurgical experts at the College of Aeronautics, Cranfield, undertook to study the problem, and as a result a series of experiments were put in hand which eventually led to a satisfactory explanation of the cause of the phenomenon. The experiments were made in the Department of Materials by Mr. A. R. Sollars under the direction of Professor A. J. Kennedy. Professor A. J. Murphy, the Principal of the College and himself a metallurgist, took an active part in the study of the problem.

A bowl belonging to the first half of the sixteenth century was chosen for the first tests. This bowl, which is described in detail in Chapter 7, was very suitable for the study because it has a large proportion of split wires which are easily visible, the original gilding having largely disappeared. The first tests were to examine areas of the bowl under a high magnification, both visually and photographically.

APPENDIX 2

The illustration of Plate 8 shows an area of this bowl (linear magnification about 4) in which about half of the wires are seen to be split. Photomicrographs with a higher magnification show the splitting of the wires in more detail. In Plate 9, with a linear magnification of about 30, we see that the wire in the centre of the picture is split over its whole length, while in the wire above the crack comes to an end some distance from the end of the wire. The right-hand wire is not split at all. Traces of enamel can be seen inside the cracks. This phenomenon is seen much more clearly in Colour Plate A (linear magnification about 17), in which there is a good deal of enamel inside the cracks. In some places this enamel, as well as the enamel along the edges of the wires is seen to be coloured red. The red colour is undoubtedly caused by copper from the wires being absorbed by the enamel. The effect is analogous to the copper-red glaze on porcelain generally known by the term *sang de boeuf*, one of the most elusive of the felspathic glazes, in which the composition of the glaze and the firing conditions require very careful control to give a good colour. The scientific explanation of the formation of these red glazes, made in China centuries before they were made in Europe, was first given by Mellor.[1]

The observations also showed that solder had run up round the edges of the wires, sometimes covering cracks on the edges of the wires and rendering them invisible. It would seem that the temperature of firing of the enamel was sufficiently high to melt some of the excess solder left on the base of the piece and cause it to run up through the enamel.

The presence of enamel inside the cracks in the wires shows that the wires were split before the piece was enamelled. The cracks indicate a failure in the material of a kind familiar to metallurgists and suggested that the splitting occurred during the manufacture of the wires from brass ingots. The method of manufacture was probably to hammer the ingots in successive stages down to thin sheet from which the wires were cut. During the hammering the metal would become hard and brittle and would tend to split. In modern practice the metal would be carefully annealed after each hammering in order to prevent the splitting. Although the Chinese were almost certainly familiar with the process of annealing, it is unlikely that they would give the careful detailed treatment necessary to prevent the splitting altogether. In the preparation of the wires by the Chinese it seems likely that visible cracks in the wires had not actually occurred when the wires were cut and placed in position, for surely any wires obviously defective would have been discarded. But any weakness in the wire might very well be revealed by splitting during the heating operations, first during the soldering and then during the firing of the enamels.

These are conjectures as to what actually happened and they clearly need experimental support. It was first necessary to show that the splitting of the wires is real and not the apparent result of doubling the

[1] J. W. Mellor, 'The chemistry of the Chinese copper-red glazes', *Transactions of the Ceramic Society*, Vol. XXXV, 1936.

APPENDIX 2

wires in some way. The regularity of the cracks made it difficult for some people, including some very competent engineers, to believe that they could be other than the result of manipulation by craftsmen. It was decided therefore to grind the surface of some of the split wires to show that the cracks are limited in depth. For this purpose a second bowl, decorated with phoenixes amid flower scrolls outside (Pl. 41B) and an archaic dragon surrounded by formal borders inside, was chosen. This bowl is of mid-sixteenth century date. Several wires on the base were ground down in successive stages. Some of the apparent cracks were found to be spaces between the wires and the surrounding solder but there were a number of true cracks in the wires and in most of these the grooves were relatively shallow and were removed by one or more grinding operations. Thus the experiments showed conclusively that there was no question of the wires having been bent over or doubled in any way.

The splitting of the wires being established, a further test was made to see if the cracks could be imitated by making wires from an ingot in a manner similar to that which, it is thought, was adopted by the ancient craftsmen. A brass ingot was hammered into a flat sheet in successive stages. When the metal was frequently annealed between the cold hammering, thin strip was produced without any splitting. If, however, during the early stages of the operation, the material was annealed, beaten to the point where cracking was just visible and then re-annealed and beaten so that no further cracking occurred, the strip showed a transverse fault. The crack first formed at an angle of 45° and did not extend very far along the length of the material. Further annealing and hammering extended the crack as the material thinned. If the resulting strip was then cut into lengths whose width corresponded to the height of the wires, longitudinal cracks were visible in the wire, the cracks being positioned anywhere across the wire. In fact, the laboratory experiment reproduced closely the kind of splitting that is actually found in the wires of Ming cloisonné pieces.

A final experiment was made to see if evidence could be found of the use of annealing in the wires of actual pieces. A wire was ground, etched and examined under the microscope. A photomicrograph, with a linear magnification of 250, showed the presence of twinning, a phenomenon associated with cold working and annealing.

The conclusions reached from this series of experiments fully confirm the conjecture that the Ming craftsmen made the wires for cloisonné by hammering out sheets of bronze from ingots and cutting the sheets into lengths of the required width. The metal was hammered out in a cold condition and annealed between the hammering operations. The presence of cracks in the wires is caused by over-working between successive annealings or inadequate annealing during one or more of the intervals. The cracks may well have been difficult to see with the naked eye and may have opened up during the heating that took place in the soldering and enamelling.

Bibliography

Enamels in General
H. H. Cunynghame, *Art enamelling on metals*, 1901.
L. F. Day, *Enamelling*, 1907.
H. Maryon, *Metalwork and enamelling*, 1954.
E. F. Strange, 'Enamel' (article in *Encyclopaedia Britannica*), 1947.

Western Asiatic and European Enamels
A. Alföldi, 'Die Goldkanne von St. Maurice d'Agaune', *Zeitschrift für Schweizerische Archaeologie und Kunstgeschichte*, 1947.
C. R. Ashbee, *The treatises of Benvenuto Cellini on metal work and sculpture, made into English from the Italian of the Marcian Codex*, 1898.
M. van Berchem and J. Strzygowski, *Amida*, 1910.
H. Buchthal, 'A note on enamelled Islamic metal work and its influence on the Latin west', *Ars Islamica*, Vols. XI, XII, 1946.
T. Burton-Brown, *Early Mediterranean migrations*, 1959.
H. H. Cunynghame, *European enamels*, 1906.
O. M. Dalton, *Byzantine art and archaeology*, 1911.
O. M. Dalton, *Catalogue of ivories, enamels, etc. in the McClean bequest, Fitzwilliam Museum*, 1912.
H. Frankfort, *The art and architecture of the ancient orient*, 1954.
M.-M. S. Gauthier, *Emaux limousins champlevés des XIIe, XIIIe et XIVe siècles*, 1950.
W. L. Hildburgh, *Mediaeval Spanish enamels*, 1936.
George H. McFadden, 'A late Cypriot III tomb from Kourion Kaloriziki No. 40,', *American Journal of Archaeology*, Vol. LVIII, 1954.
M. Rosenberg, *Geschichte der Goldschmeide-kunst auf technischer Grundlage, Zellenschmelz*, 1921–4.
M. Rostovtzeff, *Iranians and Greeks in South Russia*, 1922.
E. Rupin, *L'oeuvre de Limoges*, 1890.
Theophilus, *Diversarum artium schedula*, translated with notes by Robert Hendrie, 1847.
T. B. L. Webster, *From Mycenae to Homer*, 1959.

Chinese and Japanese Enamels
W. G. Audsley, *Notes on Japanese art*, 1874.
Dorothy Blair, 'The cloisonné-backed mirror in the Shosoin', *Journal of Glass Studies*, Vol. II (Corning Glass Centre), 1960.

BIBLIOGRAPHY

J. L. Bowes, *Japanese enamels*, 1886.
J. L. Bowes, *Handbook to the Bowes Museum of Japanese Art Work*, 1894.
J. L. Bowes, *Notes on Shippo*, 1895.
E. Bretschneider, *Mediaeval researches from far eastern Asiatic sources*, 1910.
F. Brinkley, *Japan and China*, Vol. 7, 1904.
S. W. Bushell, *Oriental ceramic art*, 1899.
S. W. Bushell, *Description of Chinese pottery and porcelain, being a translation of the T'ao Shuo*, 1910.
S. W. Bushell, *Chinese art, Vol. II* (2nd Edition), 1909, 1910.
S. W. Bushell, *Chinese art, Vol. I* (2nd Edition), 1909, 1911, 1914.
R. M. Chait, 'Some comments on the dating of early Chinese enamels', *Oriental Art*, Vol. III, No. 2, 1950.
Lady David, *Ch'ing enamelled wares in the Percival David Foundation*, 1958.
Sir Percival David, 'The Shōsō-in', *Transactions and Proceedings of the Japan Society*, Vol. XXVIII, 1932.
J. LeRoy Davidson, 'The origin and early use of the ju-i', *Artibus Asiae*, Vol. XIII, 1950.
J. J. M. de Groot, *The religious system of China*, Vol. III, 1897.
Soulié de Morant, *L'histoire de l'art chinois*, 1928.
John C. Ferguson, *Survey of Chinese art*, 1939.
C. P. Fitzgerald, *China, a short cultural history*, 1954.
H. C. Gallois, 'About T'ang and Ta Ts'in', *O.C.S. Transactions*, 1936.
H. M. Garner, 'The use of imported and native cobalt in Chinese blue and white', *Oriental Art*, Vol. II, No. 2, 1956.
H. M. Garner, *The arts of the Ming dynasty, (Metal work, including enamels)*, 1958.
J. Getz and W. H. Goodyear, *Catalogue of the Avery Collection of ancient Chinese cloisonnés, Museum of the Brooklyn Institute*, 1912.
Herbert A. Giles, *History of Chinese pictorial art*, 1905.
Basil Gray, 'The influence of near eastern metalwork on Chinese ceramics', *O.C.S. Transactions*, 1941–2.
S. Howard Hansford, *A glossary of Chinese art and archaeology*, 1954.
F. Hirth, *China and the Roman orient*, 1885.
F. Hirth and W. W. Rockhill, *Chau Ju-kua, his work on the Chinese and Arab trade in the twelfth and thirteenth centuries, entitled Chu-fan-chï*, 1912.
R. L. Hobson, 'On Chinese cloisonné enamels', *Burlington Magazine*, 1912.
Soame Jenyns, 'The problem of Chinese cloisonné enamels', *O.C.S. Transactions*, 1949-50, Vol. 25.
Soame Jenyns, *Ming pottery and porcelain*, 1953.
H. L. Joly and K. Tomita, *Japanese art and handicraft*, 1916.
B. Laufer, *Jade, a study of Chinese archaeology and religion*, 1912.

BIBLIOGRAPHY

B. Laufer, *Beginnings of porcelain in China*, 1917.

L. Olschki, *Guillame Boucher, a French artist at the court of the Khans*, 1946.

M. Paléologue, *L'art chinois*, 1887.

John A. Pope, *Chinese porcelains from the Ardebil Shrine*, 1956.

B. W. Robinson, *The arts of the Japanese sword*, 1961.

W. W. Rockhill, *The journey of Friar William of Rubruck to the eastern parts of the world*, 1900.

C. G. Seligman and H. C. Beck, 'Far eastern glass: some western origins', *M.F.E.A. Bulletin*, No. 10, 1938.

Illustrated Catalogue of Chinese Government exhibits for the International Exhibition of Chinese Art in London, Vol. IV, 1937.

Catalogue of the International Exhibition of Chinese Art, 1935–6.

Exhibition of the arts of the Ming dynasty, Detroit Institute of Arts, 1952.

The arts of the Ming dynasty, Oriental Ceramic Society, 1958.

Chinese art treasures. An exhibition of objects from the Chinese National Palace Museum and the Chinese National Central Museum, Taichung, Taiwan, 1961–2.

Index of Authors

Alföldi, 21, 114
Ashbee, 16, 114
Audsley, 114

Bank, A. V., 24
Berchem and Strzygowski, van, 23, 114
Blair, 30, 96, 98, 114
Bouillard, 71
Bowes, 100, 103, 104, 105, 115
Brankston, 91
Bretschneider, 34, 115
Brinkley, 103–4, 115
Brunton, 17
Buchthal, 25, 114
Burton-Brown, 20, 114
Bushell, 31, 32, 34, 35, 50, 61, 68, 70, 87, 88, 106, 107, 115

Cammann, 71, 83
Cecchelli, 22
Chait, 98, 115
Cunynghame, 48, 114

Dalton, 25, 114
David, Lady, 87, 96, 115
David, Sir Percival, 31, 32, 68, 97, 99, 115
Davidson, 84, 115
Day, 99, 114
de Groot, 71, 115
de Morant, 35, 88, 115
de Morgan, 17

Ferguson, 33, 115
Fitzgerald, 61, 115
Frankfort, 19, 114

Gallois, 30, 72, 97, 115
Garner, 41, 51, 107, 115
Gauthier, 13, 15, 25, 114
Getz and Goodyear, 115

Giles, 83, 115
Gray, 29, 33, 74, 99, 115

Hackenbroch, 22
Hansford, 115
Hendrie, 23, 114
Hildburgh, 25, 114
Hirth, 29, 115
Hobson, 81, 82, 97, 109, 115

Imbault-Huart, 71

Jenyns, 28, 53, 62, 70, 72, 74, 80, 115
Joly and Tomita, 102, 115

Laufer, 29, 83, 115, 116

Maryon, 18, 114
McFadden, 18, 114
Mellor, 112
Migeon, 24
Moss, 19

Olschki, 32, 116

Paléologue, 34, 116
Pope, 70, 116

Rice, D. S., 39
Robinson, 101, 116
Rockhill, 29, 32, 34, 115, 116
Rosenberg, 18, 114
Rostovtzeff, 20, 21, 114
Rupin, 25, 114

Theophilus, 23, 99, 114

Umehara, 30

Watson, 28, 100
Webster, 19, 114
Winkworth, 62

Subject Index

Added bases, 62
Addis, 71
adhesives, 45, 99, 104
annealing, 45, 112–13
Ardebil, 70
Asuka, 96

base materials, 41, 51
basse taille, 26, 94
Bolat (P'u-la), 34
brass and bronze, 41–2
British Museum, 76, 82
Buchier, 33–4
Buddhist stele, 84
Buddhist temples, 37, 57, 81, 88, 92
Byzantine enamels, 21–3, 32, 34, 98

calligraphy, 65, 107, 108
camaïeu, 26
Canton enamels, 16, 38
carnelian, 14, 17
Carolingian work, 21–2
cast bases, 41–2, 51, 53
Cellini, 16, 33
Celtic enamels, 20–1
champlevé, 15–16, 21, 40, 56, 93, 102
Chêng Ho, 61
Chinese Imperial Collection, 60, 64, 65
Ching-t'ai lan, 61
Ching-tê Chên, 59, 68, 78, 79, 87–8
cloison, 15
cloisonné (definition), 15
cloisonné on porcelain, 106
cobalt, 14, 17–19, 51, 58
College of Aeronautics, 44, 111
composition of enamels, 47
'copies of Ming', 43, 95
copper wires, 89, 90

decoration, subjects of
  archaistic motives (*t'ao t'ieh*), 56, 62, 64, 81, 88, 91
  background scrolls, 38, 39, 50, 63, 68, 70, 73
  Buddhist emblems, 57, 69, 70
  Buddhist lion-dogs, 69, 70, 89, 90, 102
  ch'i-lin, 73, 74
  cloud borders, 53, 56
  double-lined scrolls, 55, 56
  cranes, 72, 73
  dragons, 54, 55, 62, 70, 73, 76, 81, 82, 85, 86
  dragons, foliated, 70, 71
  figures of animals, 83, 92
  figures of birds, 83, 92
  fishes in waves, 70
  flower scrolls, 54, 58, 64, 88, 90
  fruiting sprays, 72
  fungus scrolls, 53
  galloping horses, 69, 86
  grape vines, 58, 64, 72
  human figures, 93
  'hundred deer', 93
  landscapes with figures, 75, 76, 82
  landscapes without figures, 64, 72, 76, 81, 82, 105
  lotus flowers, 58, 63
  lotus scrolls, 38, 50, 53–8, 62, 69, 81, 91
  lotus seed-pods, 53, 57
  mallows, 75
  mandarin ducks, 72
  parrots, 72
  phoenixes, 81
  petal borders, 53
  persimmons, 58
  pomegranates, 58
  shou character, 76, 85
  'three friends', 69, 74
  three rams, 56
  vajra, 57, 69, 70
  wave border, 54
Dōnin, 101
Double-lined characters, 54, 109

Egyptian inlays, 17
enamel (definition), 13
Eumorfopoulos Collection, 74
export of cloisonné, 38

fa hua, 59
Fa Lan, 33
famille rose, 27, 88
Fo-lang, 31, 32, 33
Freer Gallery of Art, 84, 88

garnet, 14, 17
German enamels, 25, 34
gliding, 43, 52, 90, 111
glass
  Chinese, 28
  Egyptian, 17

SUBJECT INDEX

Japanese, 96
Korean, 96
Mesopotamian, 14
Mycenaean, 17, 18
Roman, 21
stained, 25
Greek enamels, 19
grisaille, 26

Hausmaler, 27
Hermitage, Leningrad, 88
Hirado ware, 102
Hirata family, 100–2

imitations of Ming, 95
India, 37
interregnum, 60
Islamic enamels, 23–4, 32

jasper, 17
jewellery, 14–17, 94, 95

Kaji Tsunekichi, 104
Kennedy, 44
Kitson Collection, 56, 70
Ko ku yao lun, 31–5, 38, 53
Kuban enamels, 20

Lamaist ritual, 57
lapis lazuli, 14, 17, 18
Limoges enamels, 24, 25, 33
liu-li (p'i-liu-li), 29
Lombardic work, 22

Mañjuśrī (Wen Shu), 84
Marco Polo, 32
marks, general, 39, 107–10
millefiori, 21
'Ming pink', 46, 69, 90
Ming tombs, 71
mixed colours, 46, 47, 49, 51, 52, 58, 59, 80, 81
Mohammedan blue, 46, 51, 58
muffle kilns, 68
Murphy, 44
musen-shippó, 105
Mycenaean enamels, 15–19

Namikawa Yasusuki, 105
Narihisa, 101
Narisuke, 101
Nariyuki, 101
Needham, 31, 45
niello, 19, 30

Ortokid dish, 23–6, 35, 38, 47
Otto II, 25

p'ai lou, 71
painted enamels, 13, 16, 26, 94
Peking, 40, 68, 80, 87, 88, 92
Père d'Entrecolles, 87, 107

Pettitot, 27
Philostratus, 20
pin-holes, 52
plique à jour, 106

reigns (Ming and Ch'ing)
  Yung-lo, 60
  Hsüan-tê, 50, 60, 63, 66
  Chêng-t'ung, 61
  Ching-t'ai, 61
  T'ien-shun, 61
  Ch'êng-hua, 55, 60, 61, 63, 71
  Chêng-tê, 74
  Chia-ching, 67, 79
  Lung-ch'ing, 67
  Wan-li, 67, 79, 105, 109
  T'ien-ch'i, 79, 82
  Ch'ung-chêng, 79
  K'ang-hsi, 78, 79, 85–9, 109
  Yung-chêng, 88, 89, 110
  Ch'ien-lung, 34, 48, 56, 91
reign marks
  Chih-chêng, 34, 35
  Chih-yüan, 35
  Hsüan-te, 53–5, 58, 59, 66, 75, 108, 109
  Ching-t'ai, 39, 55–7, 60, 62–5, 70, 75, 81, 83, 108
  Chia-ching, 73, 109
  Wan-li, 54, 67, 75, 76, 78, 81, 82, 109
  K'ang-hsi, 88
  Ch'ien-lung, 91, 92, 95, 109–10
repoussé, 15, 93, 94
Rice, D. S., 24
Royal Ontario Museum, 84

Salting, 91
sang de boeuff, 44, 112
Sarmatians, 20, 25
Scythians, 20
shapes of cloisonné
  arm rest, 82
  beaker (*ku*), 56, 62–4, 81
  bowl, 69, 70, 94, 95, 105
  bowl-stand, 53, 54
  box, 53, 57, 58, 72, 76, 85, 91, 93, 104
  chüeh, 57
  crucifix, 100
  cup-stand, 53, 54
  disc, 53
  dish, 64, 71–3, 76, 81, 82, 104
  door handle, 100
  ewer, 74, 75, 86
  faceted vase, 75
  ice box, 92
  incense burner (general), 51, 92
  incense burner (*kuei*), 56, 62, 69, 74
  incense burner (ram), 91
  incense burner (*ting*), 42, 56, 74, 81, 91
  jar, 54
  ju-i sceptre, 83, 85, 92
  leys jar (*cha tou*), 64, 70

SUBJECT INDEX

mei p'ing, 75
moon vase, 82
panel, 82, 93
pricket candlestick, 72, 81, 85, 92
sprinkler (*kundika*), 57
stand, 86
sword guard, 100–2
temple vessel, 38, 77, 81, 88, 92
tankard, 91
vase (general), 88, 91, 93–5, 104
vase (*hu*), 81, 91
vase (*tsun*), 58
shippō, 100
Shōsō-in, 30, 84, 96–8
Shōsō-in mirror, 97–9, 102
shotai-shippō, 106
Sōken Kishō, 100
solder, 45, 46, 49, 52, 65, 99, 104
Sollars, 44
Spanish enamels, 25
split wires, 44, 45, 69, 111–13
Summer Palace, 92
Syrian work, 19

T'ang enamels, 30
T'ang Ying, 68
Ta-shih, 30–2
Ta Ts'in, 29

Tea ceremony, 103
Theophano, 25
Tibet, 37, 38, 57
T'ien-kung k'ai wu 45
Toutin, 26, 27
Transitional period, 79–81
Ts'ao Chao, 31
Tsao-pan Ch'u, 87
turquoise, 14, 17

University of Pennsylvania Museum, Philadelphia, 89, 90

vajra, 56, 57, 69
Victoria and Albert Museum, 22, 75, 76, 82, 105

Wang Tso, 31
Wei lio, 29
William of Rubruck, 32–4
wire-drawing, 43–5, 49, 80

Yüan dynasty, 31, 32–6, 38, 50, 54
Yukimitsu, 101
Yung-ho-kung, 88
Yunnan, 31–2

zinc, introduction of, 41

1. EGYPTIAN, XII DYNASTY (c. 1800 B.C.). WIDTH 3·2 in.
Metropolitan Museum of Art, New York
See p. 17

2. MYCENAEAN, TWELFTH CENTURY B.C.
WIDTH OF SPHERE 1·2 in.
Nicosia Museum, Cyprus
See p. 18

3. CAROLINGIAN, NINTH CENTURY A.D.
HEIGHT 11·9 in.
St. Maurice d'Agaune Monastery
See p. 21

4A. BYZANTINE, ELEVENTH CENTURY. WIDTH 1·5 in.
Victoria and Albert Museum
See pp. 22, 98

4B. BYZANTINE, ELEVENTH CENTURY. HEIGHT 4·1 in.
Victoria and Albert Museum
See pp. 22, 98

5A. JAPANESE, SEVENTEENTH CENTURY OR LATER
DIAMETER 7·2 in.
Shōsō-in, Nara, Japan
See pp. 30, 97–9, 102

5B, C. POSSIBLY CHINESE, T'ANG DYNASTY OR LATER
DIAMETER 3·0 in.
Kyoto Archaeological Museum, Japan
See p. 30

6. ISLAMIC, EARLY TWELFTH CENTURY. DIAMETER 9·1 in.
Tiroler Landesmuseum Ferdinandeum, Innsbruck
See p. 23

7. ISLAMIC, TWELFTH CENTURY. REVERSE OF PLATE 6

8. DETAIL OF SIXTEENTH CENTURY CHINESE BOWL

9. DETAIL OF SIXTEENTH CENTURY CHINESE BOWL
Linear magnification ×30
See pp. 44–5, 111–13

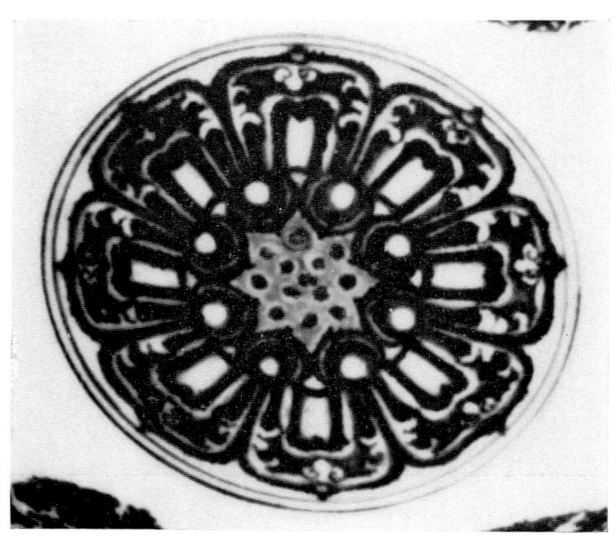

10A. HSÜAN-TÊ MARK AND PERIOD. DIAMETER 6·5 in.
Sir Percival and Lady David
See pp. 53, 57

10B. DETAIL OF FIFTEENTH CENTURY BLUE AND WHITE BOWL
Chinese Imperial Collection, Taiwan
See p. 53

11 A, B. HSÜAN-TÊ MARK AND PERIOD. DIAMETER 4·8 in.
Dr. P. Uldry
See p. 53

12. HSÜAN-TÊ MARK, FIFTEENTH CENTURY. HEIGHT 25·0 in.
British Museum
See pp. 54–5

13 A, B, C. DETAILS OF JAR IN PLATE 12
See pp. 54–5

14. FIRST HALF, FIFTEENTH CENTURY. WIDTH 8·1 in.
Victoria and Albert Museum
See pp. 56, 69

15. FIRST HALF, FIFTEENTH CENTURY. WIDTH 13·7 in.
Musée des Arts Decoratifs
See pp. 55–6

16. FIRST HALF, FIFTEENTH CENTURY. HEIGHT 8·0 in.
ex Kitson Collection
See p. 57

17A. FIRST HALF, FIFTEENTH CENTURY. WIDTH 5·8 in.
ex Kitson Collection
See p. 56

17B. FIRST HALF, FIFTEENTH CENTURY. WIDTH 6·0 in.
Victoria and Albert Museum
See p. 57

18. FIRST HALF, FIFTEENTH CENTURY. HEIGHT 8·8 in.
See p. 56

19A. FIRST HALF, FIFTEENTH CENTURY. WIDTH 7·1 in.
ex Kitson Collection
See p. 56

19B. FIRST HALF, FIFTEENTH CENTURY. DIAMETER 4·8 in.
Mr. and Mrs. A. S. de Breyne
See p. 57

20. FIRST HALF, FIFTEENTH CENTURY. HEIGHT 11·0 in.
Mrs. Walter Sedgwick
See p. 57

21A. FIRST HALF, FIFTEENTH CENTURY. WIDTH 6·3 in.
Victoria and Albert Museum
See pp. 56, 69

21B. FIFTEENTH CENTURY. WIDTH 8·4 in.
See pp. 56–7

22. HSÜAN-TÊ MARK, FIFTEENTH CENTURY. DIAMETER 7·5 in.
Mrs. Walter Sedgwick
See pp. 53–4

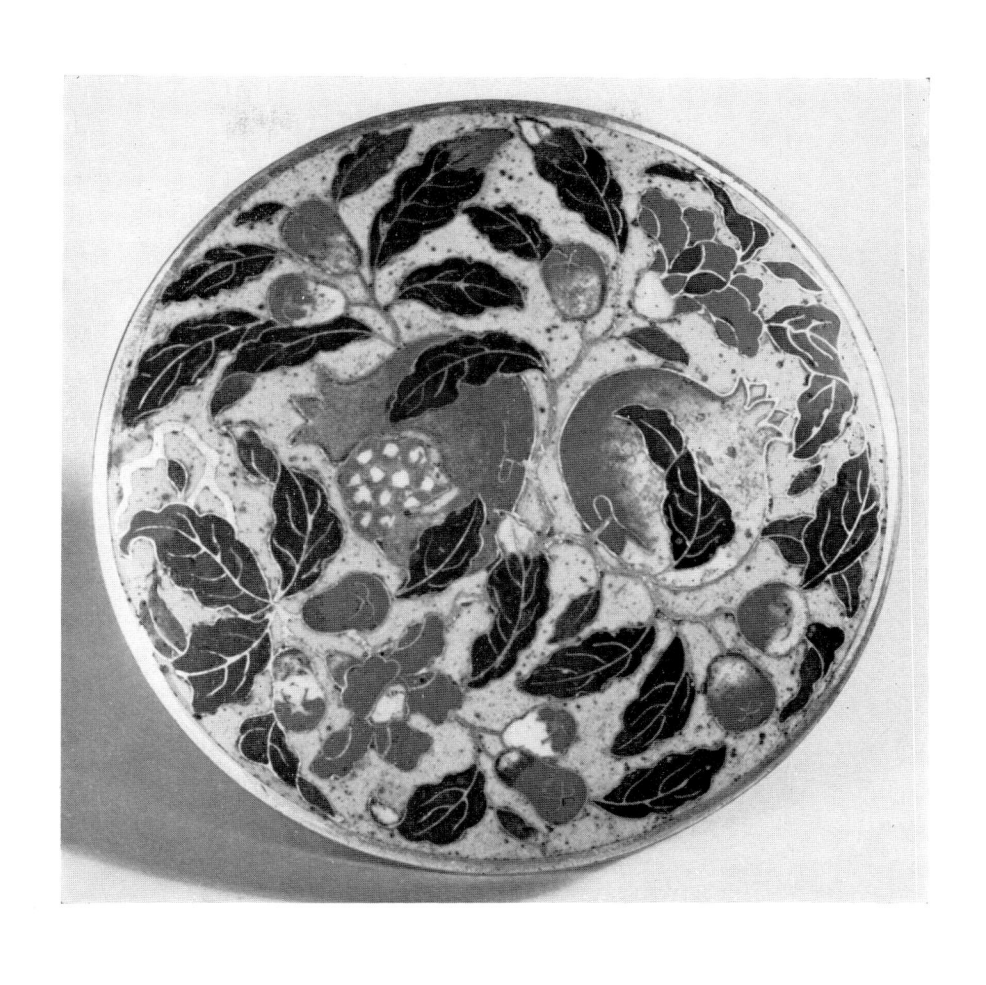

23. SECOND HALF, FIFTEENTH CENTURY. DIAMETER 4·7 in.
Lord Cunliffe
See p. 58

24. SECOND HALF, FIFTEENTH CENTURY. DIAMETER 4·6 in.
Musée des Arts Decoratifs
See p. 58

25. SECOND HALF, FIFTEENTH CENTURY. HEIGHT 9·8 in.
See p. 58

26A. SECOND HALF, FIFTEENTH CENTURY. DIAMETER 3·3 in.
26B. SECOND HALF, FIFTEENTH CENTURY. DIAMETER 4·7 in.
Fenton House, National Trust
See p. 58

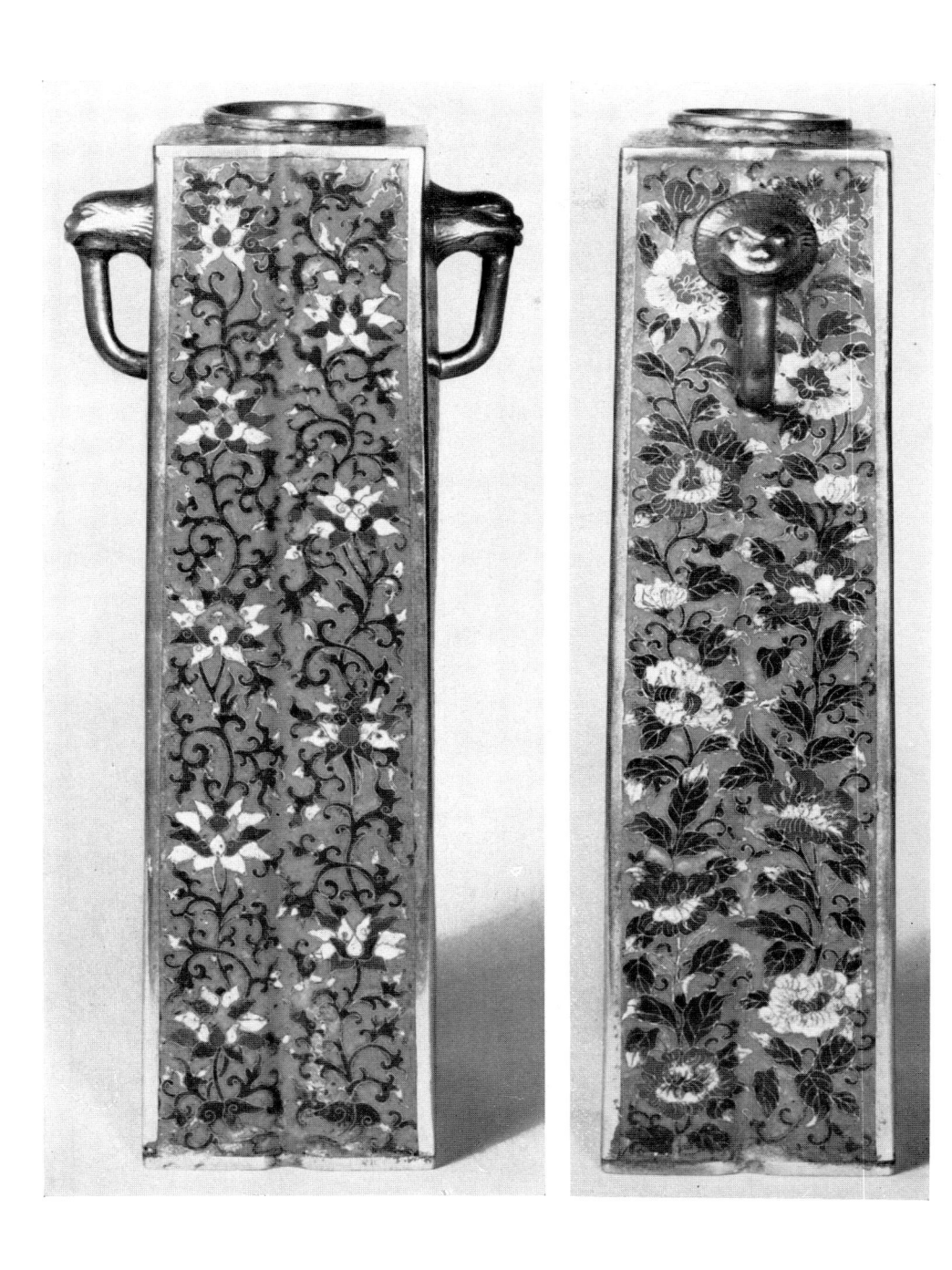

27 A, B. LATE FIFTEENTH CENTURY. HEIGHT 9·4 in.
See p. 58

28. LATE FIFTEENTH CENTURY. HEIGHT 16·5 in.
Mr. and Mrs. Soame Jenyns
See pp. 58–9

29. LATE FIFTEENTH CENTURY. HEIGHT 13·5 in.
Percival David Foundation
See pp. 58–9

30A. EARLY SIXTEENTH CENTURY. WIDTH 11·3 in.
Mr. Paul Getty
See pp. 56, 69, 74

30B. EARLY SIXTEENTH CENTURY. DIAMETER 6·4 in.
See p. 69

31A. EARLY SIXTEENTH CENTURY. DIAMETER 9·6 in.
Mme. D. Lyon-Goldschmidt
See pp. 70–1

31B. FIRST HALF, SIXTEENTH CENTURY. DIAMETER 8·5 in.
See pp. 44, 69, 111–13

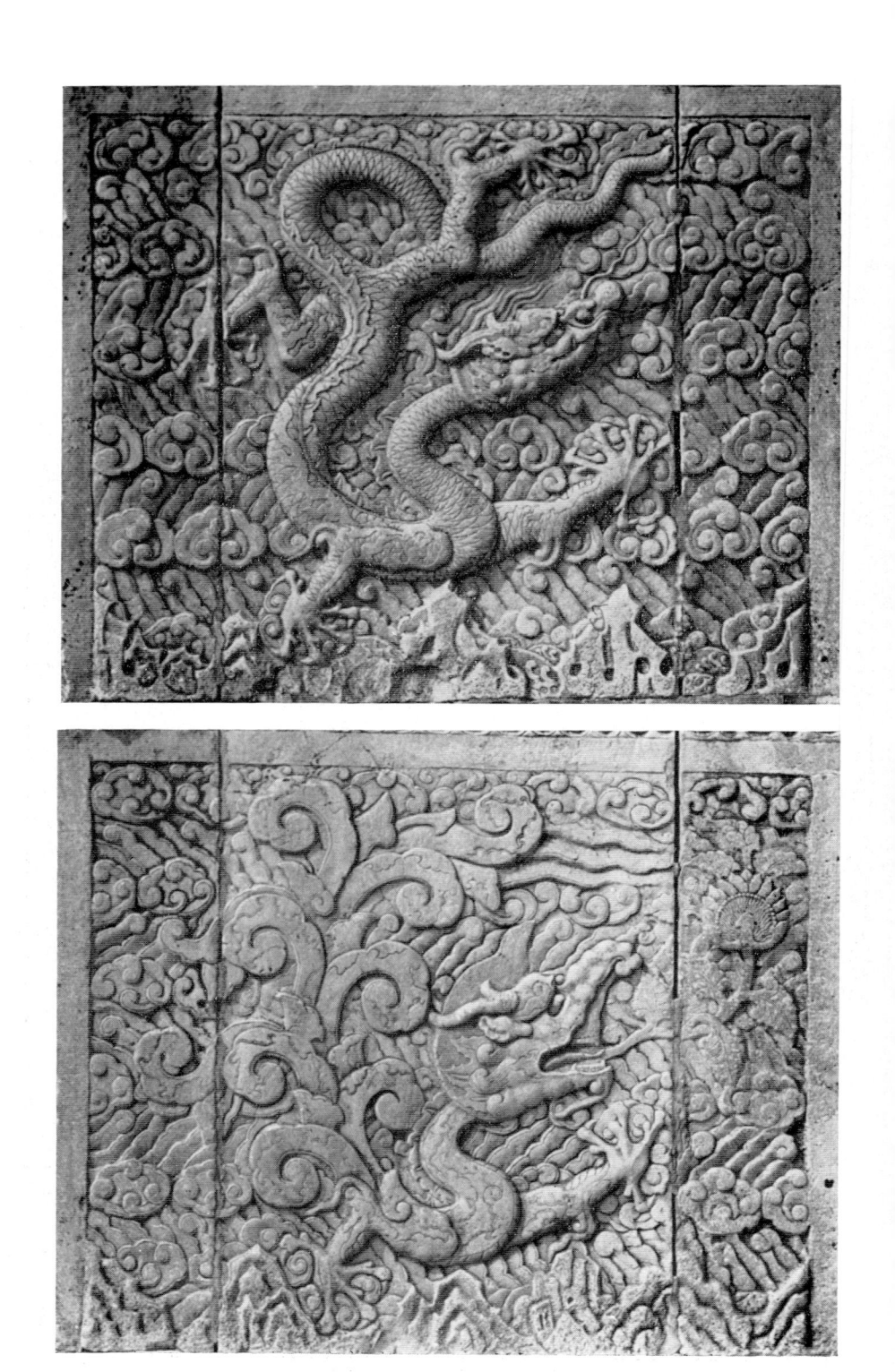

32 A, B. EARLY SIXTEENTH CENTURY
See p. 71

33. EARLY SIXTEENTH CENTURY. HEIGHT 7·1 in.
ex Kitson Collection
See p. 70

34. FIRST HALF, SIXTEENTH CENTURY. DIAMETER 6·8 in.
Gemeente Museum, The Hague
See p. 72

35. FIRST HALF, SIXTEENTH CENTURY. DIAMETER 6·6 in.
ex Kitson Collection
See p. 72

36. FIRST HALF, SIXTEENTH CENTURY. DIAMETER 8·1 in.
See p. 72

37. FIRST HALF, SIXTEENTH CENTURY. DIAMETER 6·7 in.
Musée des Arts Decoratifs
See p. 72

38 A, B. CHIA-CHING MARK, MID-SIXTEENTH CENTURY
DIAMETER 8·9 in.
Dr. P. Uldry
See p. 73

39A. MID-SIXTEENTH CENTURY. HEIGHT 8·8 in.
Victoria and Albert Museum
See p. 74

39B. CHIA-CHING MARK, MID-SIXTEENTH CENTURY
DIAMETER 9·3 in.
Musée des Arts Decoratifs
See p. 73

40 A, B. FIRST HALF, SIXTEENTH CENTURY. DIAMETER 3·9 in.
Victoria and Albert Museum
See pp. 39, 72

40C. MID-SIXTEENTH CENTURY. WIDTH 5·0 in.
Mr. John Levy
See pp. 56, 74

41A. FIRST HALF, SIXTEENTH CENTURY. HEIGHT 4·6 in.
Musée des Arts Decoratifs
See p. 70

41B. MID-SIXTEENTH CENTURY. DIAMETER 4·9 in.
See p. 113

41C. MID-SIXTEENTH CENTURY. WIDTH 4·7 in.
Victoria and Albert Museum
See p. 74

42. MID-SIXTEENTH CENTURY. HEIGHT 12·9 in.
See pp. 74–5

43. SECOND HALF, SIXTEENTH CENTURY. HEIGHT 10·0 in.
See p. 75

44A. FIRST HALF, SIXTEENTH CENTURY. HEIGHT 8·0 in. *Musée des Arts Decoratifs.* See p. 75

44B. FIRST HALF, SIXTEENTH CENTURY. HEIGHT 8·0 in. *ex Kitson Collection.* See p. 75

45. SECOND HALF, SIXTEENTH CENTURY. WIDTH 20·7 in.
Musée des Arts Decoratifs
See p. 75

46. SECOND HALF, SIXTEENTH CENTURY. HEIGHT 11·0 in.
Chinese Imperial Collection, Taiwan
See p. 64

47 A, B. WAN-LI MARK AND PERIOD. DIAMETER 4·0 in.
Sir Percival and Lady David
See p. 76

47C. WAN-LI MARK AND PERIOD ON DISH (Col. Pl. D)
British Museum
See p. 76

48. SECOND HALF, SIXTEENTH CENTURY. DIAMETER 14·2 in.
Philadelphia Museum of Art
See pp. 76, 104

49. SECOND HALF, SIXTEENTH CENTURY. DIAMETER 14·2 in.
Musée des Arts Decoratifs
See pp. 76, 104

50. EARLY SEVENTEENTH CENTURY. HEIGHT 29·5 in.
Miss A. C. Kemp
See p. 81

51A. EARLY SEVENTEENTH CENTURY. HEIGHT 10·5 in.
Miss A. C. Kemp
See p. 81

51B. EARLY SEVENTEENTH CENTURY. DIAMETER 9·4 in.
Miss A. C. Kemp
See p. 82

52. FIRST HALF, SEVENTEENTH CENTURY. HEIGHT 13·5 in.
See p. 81

53. FIRST HALF, SEVENTEENTH CENTURY. HEIGHT 15·4 in.
See p. 81

54. FIRST HALF, SEVENTEENTH CENTURY. HEIGHT 8·5 in.
See p. 82

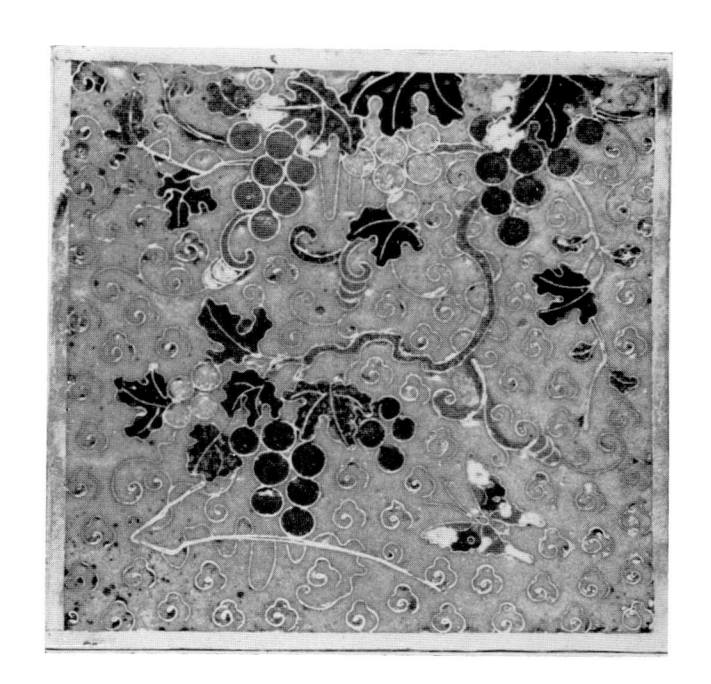

55 A, B. FIRST HALF, SEVENTEENTH CENTURY. WIDTH 5·1 in.
See p. 82

56. FIRST HALF, SEVENTEENTH CENTURY. 14·5 in. by 19·0 in.
Messrs. Spink and Son
See p. 82.

57. FIRST HALF, SEVENTEENTH CENTURY. WIDTH 14.7 in.
Mrs. Walter Sedgwick
See p. 82

58A. FIRST HALF, SEVENTEENTH CENTURY. LENGTH 6·7 in.
See p. 83

58B. FIRST HALF, SEVENTEENTH CENTURY. LENGTH 8·0 in.
Musée des Arts Decoratifs
See p. 83

59. SECOND HALF, SEVENTEENTH CENTURY. LENGTH 10·1 in.
Musée des Arts Decoratifs
See p. 83

60. SECOND HALF, SEVENTEENTH CENTURY. DIAMETER 19·5 in.
Royal Scottish Museum, Edinburgh
See pp. 81–2

61A. SECOND HALF, SEVENTEENTH CENTURY. LENGTH 16·0 in.
Miss A. C. Kemp
See pp. 83–5

61 B, C. SECOND HALF, SEVENTEENTH CENTURY
LENGTH 16·1 in.
See pp. 83–5

61 D, E. SECOND HALF, SEVENTEENTH CENTURY
DIAMETER 4·7 in.
See pp. 83–5

62A. SECOND HALF, SEVENTEENTH CENTURY. HEIGHT 9·6 in.
Miss A. C. Kemp
See p. 85

62B. SECOND HALF, SEVENTEENTH CENTURY
DIAMETER 5·6 in.
Miss A. C. Kemp
See p. 85

63A. SECOND HALF, SEVENTEENTH CENTURY
DIAMETER 4·6 in.
Miss A. C. Kemp
See p. 85

63B. SECOND HALF, SEVENTEENTH CENTURY. DIAMETER 6·8 in.
Miss A. C. Kemp
See pp. 85–6

64. SECOND HALF, SEVENTEENTH CENTURY. HEIGHT 22·0 in.
Miss A. C. Kemp
See p. 86

65. SECOND HALF, SEVENTEENTH CENTURY. HEIGHT 34·0 in.
Messrs. Spink and Son
See p. 86

66. EARLY EIGHTEENTH CENTURY. HEIGHT 12·1 in.
Freer Gallery of Art, Washington
See p. 88

67A. CH'IEN-LUNG MARK AND PERIOD. HEIGHT 3·5 in.
Victoria and Albert Museum
See p. 91

67B. CH'IEN-LUNG MARK AND PERIOD. WIDTH 5·0 in.
Victoria and Albert Museum
See p. 91

68A. CH'IEN-LUNG MARK AND PERIOD. LENGTH 7·9 in.
Victoria and Albert Museum
See p. 93

68B. CH'IEN-LUNG MARK AND PERIOD. LENGTH 8·1 in.
Victoria and Albert Museum
See p. 91

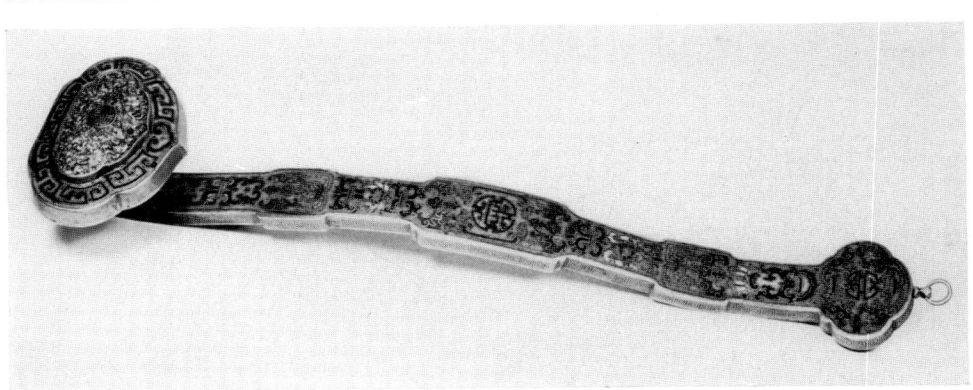

69A. CH'IEN-LUNG MARK AND PERIOD
HEIGHT OF VASE 5·2 in., DIAMETER OF BOX 3·0 in.
See p. 91

69B. CH'IEN-LUNG PERIOD. LENGTH 15·7 in.
Royal Scottish Museum, Edinburgh
See p. 92

70. CH'IEN-LUNG PERIOD
Ownership and dimensions unknown
See p. 92

71. CH'IEN-LUNG PERIOD. LENGTH 3 ft. 7.2 in.
Victoria and Albert Museum
See p. 92

72. CH'IEN-LUNG PERIOD. HEIGHT 50·0 in.
ex Kitson Collection
See p. 92

73. LATE SEVENTEENTH OR EARLY EIGHTEENTH CENTURY
HEIGHT 7 ft. 9·5 in.
University of Pennsylvania Museum, Philadelphia
See pp. 89–90

74A. CH'IEN-LUNG PERIOD. LENGTH 10·0 in.
ex Kitson Collection
See p. 92

74B. CH'IEN-LUNG PERIOD. HEIGHT 10·7 in.
ex Kitson Collection
See p. 92

75. CH'IEN-LUNG PERIOD. HEIGHT 23·7 in.
ex Mrs. Mary Neame Collection
See p. 92

76. LATE SEVENTEENTH CENTURY. HEIGHT 5·8 in.
Mr. and Mrs. R. H. R. Palmer
See p. 93

77. CH'IEN-LUNG PERIOD. 21·0 in. by 13·5 in.
Mr. S. Soames
See p. 93

78. CH'IEN-LUNG PERIOD. DIAMETER 15·2 in.
Victoria and Albert Museum
See p. 93

79. CH'IEN-LUNG PERIOD. HEIGHT 9·6 in.
Victoria and Albert Museum
See p. 93

80A. CH'IEN-LUNG PERIOD. DIAMETER 4·4 in.
Victoria and Albert Museum
See p. 94

80B. EARLY NINETEENTH CENTURY. LENGTH OF HAIRPIN 3·5 in.
Victoria and Albert Museum
See p. 95

81A. CH'IEN-LUNG MARK AND PERIOD
HEIGHT OF *chüeh* 6·0 in., DIAMETER OF STAND 7·0 in.
Mr. H. R. Milner
See p. 94

81B. CH'IEN-LUNG MARK AND PERIOD. HEIGHT 5·7 in.
British Museum
See p. 94

82 A, B. CH'IEN-LUNG PERIOD. DIAMETER OF DISH 19·5 in.
Victoria and Albert Museum
See p. 94

83A. EARLY NINETEENTH CENTURY. HEIGHT 6·5 in.
83B. EARLY NINETEENTH CENTURY. LENGTH 12·0 in.
See p. 95

84 A, B. NINETEENTH CENTURY. DIAMETER OF BOWL 8·9 in.
See p. 95

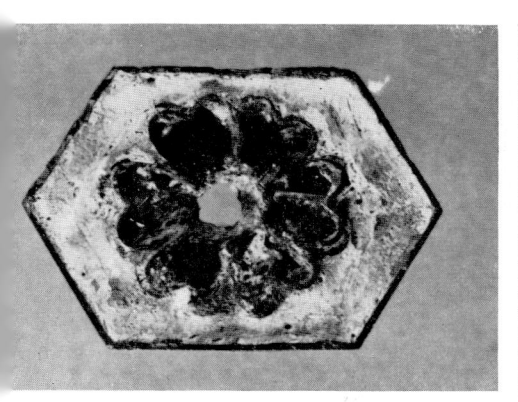

85 A, B. PROBABLY SEVENTH CENTURY A.D. WIDTH 2·0 in.
Yamato Historical Museum, Japan
See p. 96

85C. EARLY SEVENTEENTH CENTURY. HEIGHT 5·0 in.
Osaka City Museum, Japan
See p. 100

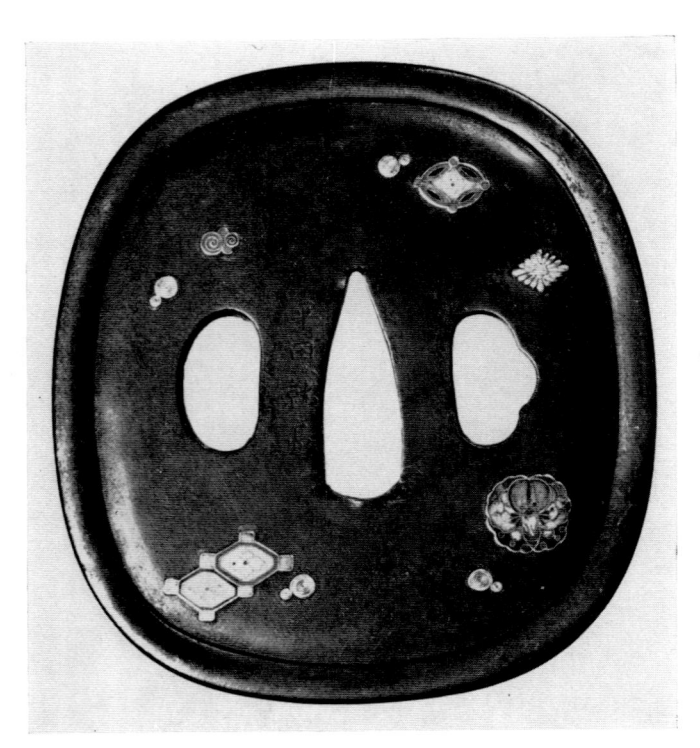

86A. EARLY NINETEENTH CENTURY. HEIGHT 3·3 in.
86B. EARLY NINETEENTH CENTURY. HEIGHT 2·6 in.
See pp. 101–2

87 A, B. EARLY NINETEENTH CENTURY. HEIGHT 3·3 in.
Victoria and Albert Museum
See p. 101

88A. EIGHTEENTH CENTURY. HEIGHT 2·8 in.

88B. EARLY EIGHTEENTH CENTURY. HEIGHT 3·1 in.
Victoria and Albert Museum

88C. POSSIBLY SEVENTEENTH CENTURY. HEIGHT 3·4 in.
Victoria and Albert Museum
See p. 102

89A. EIGHTEENTH CENTURY. HEIGHT 7·0 in.
89B. EIGHTEENTH CENTURY. DIAMETER 7·5 in.
Victoria and Albert Museum
See p. 105

90. MID-NINETEENTH CENTURY. DIAMETER 7·3 in.
See p. 104

91A. MID-NINETEENTH CENTURY. HEIGHT 8·2 in.
91B. MID-NINETEENTH CENTURY. DIAMETER 6·0 in.
See p. 104

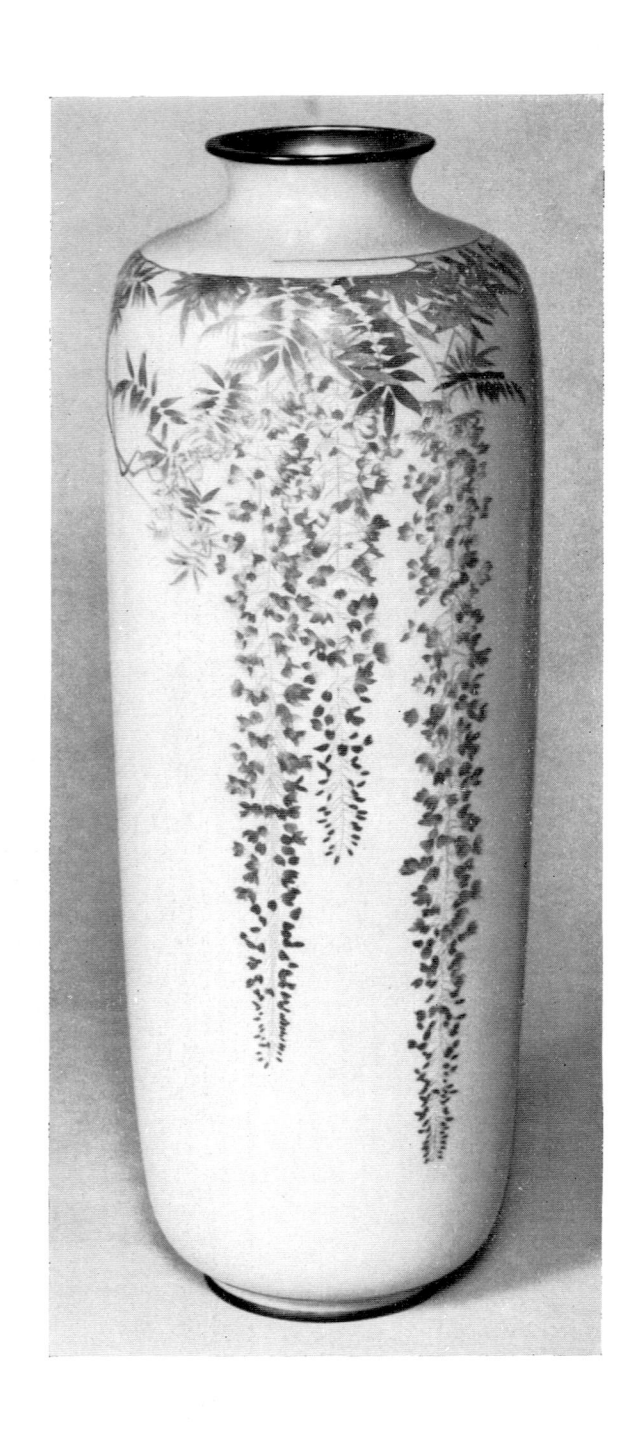

92. LATE NINETEENTH CENTURY. HEIGHT 12·1 in.
Victoria and Albert Museum
See p. 105

93A. LATE NINETEENTH CENTURY. DIAMETER 3·9 in.
Victoria and Albert Museum
See p. 106

93B. LATE NINETEENTH CENTURY. DIAMETER 7·2 in.
Victoria and Albert Museum
See p. 105

94 A, B. LATE NINETEENTH CENTURY. DIAMETER 3·1 in.
Victoria and Albert Museum
See p. 106

95A. HSÜAN-TÊ MARK ON DISH (Col. Pl. B)
95B. HSÜAN-TÊ MARK ON BLUE AND WHITE DISH
95C. HSÜAN-TÊ MARK ON BOX (Pl. 26B)
95D. CHING-T'AI MARK ON VASE (Pl. 20)
95E. HSÜAN-TÊ MARK ON CUP-STAND (Pl. 22)
95F. WAN-LI MARK
95G. CHING-T'AI MARK ON INCENSE BURNER (Pl. 21A)
95H. CHING-T'AI MARK ON INCENSE BURNER (Pl. 21B)
See pp. 107–10

96A. K'ANG-HSI MARK ON VASE (Pl. 66)
96B. CH'IEN-LUNG MARK ON CASKET (Pl. 67B)
96C. CH'IEN-LUNG MOULDED MARK
96D. CH'IEN-LUNG INCISED MARK ON VASE (Pl. 69A)
96E. CH'IEN-LUNG INCISED MARK
See pp. 107–10